A Fine Line

A Fine Line

Searching for Balance Among Mountains

Graham Zimmerman

MOUNTAINEERS
BOOKS

MOUNTAINEERS BOOKS is dedicated to the exploration, preservation, and enjoyment of outdoor and wilderness areas.

1001 SW Klickitat Way, Suite 201, Seattle, WA 98134
800-553-4453, www.mountaineersbooks.org

Printed in the United States of America
Distributed in the United Kingdom by Cordee, www.cordee.co.uk

26 25 24 23   1 2 3 4 5

Copyeditor: Theresa Winchell
Design and layout: Jen Grable
All photographs by the author unless credited otherwise
Cover photographs: *Graham Zimmerman* © Forest Woodward, *Clouds* Nitish Waila/iStock
Frontispiece: *Graham Zimmerman looking out over the Purcell Mountains of Canada* © Forest Woodward

Library of Congress Control Number: 2023932978

Mountaineers Books titles may be purchased for corporate, educational, or other promotional sales, and our authors are available for a wide range of events. For information on special discounts or booking an author, contact our customer service at 800-553-4453 or mbooks@mountaineersbooks.org.

♻ Printed on FSC-certified and 30% recycled materials

ISBN (paperback): 978-1-68051-590-9
ISBN (ebook): 978-1-68051-591-6

An independent nonprofit publisher since 1960

Contents

Author's Note

It is often said that "to be a good climber is to have a terrible memory," and this is a cliché I certainly embody. The stories told in the following chapters are the truth, but they do not represent the complete story. In telling my story, I have left out many climbs—a number of entire expeditions are excluded—not to mention other life experiences, in order to refine my story down to its most salient points. My intention is to both entertain the reader and share the philosophy that the practice of climbing and its incredible community have brought to my life. It goes without saying that my climbing partners may have had vastly different experiences during these climbs.

If you're looking for beta on specific climbs, please refer to the articles my partners and I have published in the *American Alpine Journal*, as those were written with an eye for detail and for providing others a pathway to follow the routes we opened. This book is a story meant to share the lessons I have learned from climbing—not just how to get up individual climbs but how I attempt to construct a life that balances trying new routes in the world's greatest ranges with being a responsible partner and member of society.

Keep it sharp out there, and thank you for reading.

Prologue:
On Chogori

[JULY 2021]

My body flowed through the familiar cadence of *kick, kick, punch, punch* as I bashed my crampons and tools into the ice to create purchase. The cool air was comfortable against my face and felt delicious in my lungs as I took deep breaths. I could hear the thud of Ian's crampons and tools hitting the ice 200 feet below. His rhythm mirrored my own, indicating he was in his own, similar zone. It was the middle of the night, and we were moving efficiently up the web of couloirs and snowfields leading to the crest of the West Ridge on the second-highest peak on the planet in the remote Karakoram Range.

Our goal was to climb the route with only the equipment on our backs and the rope tied between us, a style of climbing referred to as alpine style or "by fair means." Hundreds of other peaks had prepared us for this climb. We had meticulously strategized our equipment and training, allowing us the chance to make our plans a reality.

A fortuitous full moon shone down through clear skies. It cast shadows down the route's rock towers and illuminated the snow. I was climbing without a headlamp and, as we gained elevation, the

Karakoram revealed itself around us in the moonlight—eerie and majestic. I felt bewitched by its beauty.

Having run out of protection and no longer able to maintain our connection to the mountain, I stopped to build an anchor. I placed two screws in the firm ice, leaned back, and pulled the rope tight on Ian. Catching my breath in the rarefied mountain air, I thought to myself that this might be the best night I'd experienced in the mountains. *A night like this could make a trip worth it, even if we don't summit.* Then I looked to the summit, still towering nearly 10,000 feet above us.

Maybe we would be granted passage.

Two days later, I lay back on a flat ledge of rock protruding from the ridge as the hot sun bore down. My feet hung over the edge. Below them stretched out the winding crest of the West Ridge, falling away for 6,000 feet to the Savoia Glacier that wound its way down through a series of small icefalls to the Godwin Austen and then onto the mighty Baltoro. The peak we were attempting was named Karakoram Two by the Great Trigonometrical Survey, a multidecade project in the nineteenth century run by the British to map the Indian subcontinent. The peak was measured at 28,251 feet, making it the second highest on the planet, and the name was shorted simply to K2. The Balti people—the ethnic group of Tibetan descent who live near the base of the peak—know it as Chogori, or "big mountain." In a gesture of solidarity and respect, this local name is the title we decided to use to refer to the stunningly steep, triangular wedge of alpine majesty.

Looking out at the glacial systems below, I thought about the water running down the flanks of the mountain. It flows down into those giant hulks of rumbling ice and then into the Braldu River by which it is carried into the Indus. The Indus is one of the four sacred waterways that run off of Mount Kailash in Tibet, and whose flows have sustained human communities since as far back as 3300 BCE. As it crashes out of high peaks, it also draws a line of demarcation between the two highest mountain ranges on the planet—the Himalaya to the south and the Karakoram to the north. I find them to be the most imposing and splendid results of the natural processes taking place on planet Earth.

In a life in which I have never, in the traditional sense, found God, these are places that, for me, represent the holy.

My climbing partner, perched on a similar ledge just above me, was Ian Welsted, one of Canada's most experienced alpinists. His powerful frame was curled up, sound asleep, with his face coated in the opaque white of zinc oxide, protecting it from the sun's rays. Originally from the flat countryside of Manitoba, he had moved to Chamonix, France, as a teenager. Seeking steep skiing, he had instead found technical climbing and never looked back. Now, 30 years later, he had logged countless hours climbing in the world's biggest ranges and on the sheer walls and frozen waterfalls of the Canadian Rockies.

Ian and I had met seven years before, along the French and Italian border. We were both nominated as finalists for the highest honor in alpine climbing, the Piolet d'Or, an award that focuses not only on the difficulty of new routes but also on the style and ethics of the ascents. His nomination came from his first ascent, along with our friend Raphael Slawinski, of an unclimbed summit in Pakistan via its sheer northern wall. I was at the ceremony with my longtime climbing partner Mark Allen; we had been nominated for our first ascent of a striking buttress on a remote peak in Alaska. The festivities had been extravagant, with champagne and parades. Ian and I snuck away to connect more personally, more interested in talking about future projects and sampling Italian espresso.

In the end, his team won the award, and it was well deserved. We all celebrated because none of us were there to compete. Ian and I stayed in touch in the intervening years, and when I needed a partner for the West Ridge of Chogori, he was an obvious choice.

Ian was at ease in the mountains but, just like me, was surprised by the warm conditions we were experiencing.

A volley of snow and rocks roared down the slope, 300 feet to our right, and Ian looked up.

"That came directly down the couloir we want to climb up?" Ian asked.

It had.

"This is *not* good," he mumbled.

Our goal for the expedition was a first ascent of the 11,000-foot direct West Ridge of Chogori in our fast and light alpine style. We were still on the previously climbed West Ridge route, where three past teams had slowly ascended using over 20,000 feet of fixed rope to siege their way up the mountain. Each had reached just above 26,000 feet and had then taken a hard turn to the left or right, avoiding the alluring but steep direct line to the summit. The line took on a stunning gully of snow and ice threading through a series of rock towers. We wanted to improve on both the line and the style. Only one previous attempt on Chogori had come close to this goal, but the team was reported to have used previously fixed rope high on the peak. If successful, our ascent would be part of redefining what was possible on the mountain—and, more importantly, what was possible for us as individual practitioners of the art of alpinism.

To acclimate for climbing on the West Ridge, Ian and I used the most straightforward route on neighboring Broad Peak to ascend to 23,000 feet. A series of international teams had been fixing thousands of feet of rope along the route, which mostly involved walking on snow up the western flank of the mountain. It had been my first time seeing this style of siege climbing; thus far, my career had been spent chasing unclimbed routes on remote steep peaks, not nearly as tall as Chogori but more severe in their architecture. This was my inaugural climb on a well-known and well-explored peak in the Greater Ranges.

As we climbed, thin white-and-blue fixed rope lay as discarded litter next to the track. The rock outcrops along the route were covered in the trash from past seasons, years of old ropes connected to tangles of faded slings and manky pitons.

The other climbers on the mountain, who were using fixed ropes and stocked camps, seemed okay with looking past all this garbage. To my eyes, the refuse was monstrous, standing in stark contrast to the stunningly crisp undulations of gray rock and white snow that defined the 12th-highest peak on the planet. It hurt to see the mountains treated with such blatant disregard—like graffiti desecrating a sacred object. To unceremoniously leave all the trash behind, opting instead for an at-all-costs focus on the summit, denigrates the beauty of the space. It represents a very different relationship to the natural world than my own.

If only these people would open their eyes to what they are defacing, maybe then would it stop?

Just below 23,000 feet, I took the lead, punching the track upward toward the third camp on the mountain. For a moment, I was alone. The fixed lines of past seasons were buried in the snow. The steps upward in the fresh snow were a relief from the mess below. I didn't move fast, focusing rather on a steady, consistent pace. For a moment, I let myself pretend that I was not on a trade route but instead was stepping forward into the unknown. I looked to my right toward Chogolisa, its ridges rising into the sky in a form reminiscent of Hokusai's painting *The Great Wave off Kanagawa*. It was there, on that parallel peak, that Hermann Buhl had perished in 1957 after making the first ascent of Broad Peak by this very route. I thought about him and his team pushing through this same terrain toward the summit—it must have been incredible.

Climbing over a crest to a relatively flat area that housed Camp 3, the moment quickly soured. I was greeted by faded aluminum poles and ragged bits of nylon sticking out of the snow. It was a graveyard of destroyed tents left behind by past expeditions. Buhl and his team had climbed in a style not unlike our modern alpine style—without the aid of supplemental oxygen, high-altitude porters, or base camp support. It is a shame that the route has been reduced to its current state.

An hour later, while parties of other independent climbers set their tents up atop the wreck of old ones, I walked along the slope to the south, trying to get away from the refuse, but it continued across the entirety of the slope. In the end, the best I could do was carry down pieces of an old tent pulled out of the snow when we departed the following day—a small attempt to leave the mountain cleaner than I'd found it.

Back on the ledge on Chogori, I looked up at the sky, a stunning expanse of azure blue without a wisp of wind. By height, we were a little over halfway up the route. It was good progress, and climbing away from the garbage and crowds of commercial expeditions was a relief. Ian and I knew that the upper half of the mountain would be far more challenging, with thin air and steep climbing ahead. This was precisely why we had come, and I was feeling very strong and ready. But our progress had been stalled by hot temperatures and the subsequent avalanches of rock, ice, and snow.

Before the expedition, I spoke with many climbers who had spent time on Chogori. The prevailing wisdom was that above 21,000 feet, the ambient temperature of the high and dry air should be cool enough for us to climb safely during the day. Lower down on the peak, we carefully climbed during the night to avoid ascending when the temperatures peaked above freezing, unlocking the stones from above our heads and releasing them to the pull of gravity, and lubricating the snowpack, making wet avalanches another major hazard. Our plan had been a daylight ascent from this point, to make faster progress on the upper mountain. But the conditions were foiling us.

I kept my wristwatch, which included a thermometer, under an insulated jacket on the ledge so I could get an air temperature reading in the shade, without the effect of solar radiation. I pulled it out quickly, giving the digital screen a quick glance. It was a disappointing 12 degrees Celsius. Twelve degrees above freezing. It was very hot, far too hot to be climbing on a gigantic mountain composed of a frozen matrix of ice and rock—a melting matrix.

▲

ANOTHER DEADLY VOLLEY of rocks fell to our right.

We were in a safe place, on a convexity with no rocks or ice directly above us, but this would not be true on the route ahead. I carefully stood up and looked out at where the route traversed 300 feet across the south face of the peak to a meandering line of ice gullies and ice fields that led up 3,000 feet onto the upper mountain. It was within this gully that many of the rocks were pouring down the mountain.

I calculated how long it would take us to climb 3,000 feet of terrain. I compared this to the duration of climbing in the middle of the night, when the terrain would be out of the sun and cool enough to ascend safely. We would need to move significantly faster than we had on the lower mountain, where the air was thicker and we had a better handle on finding the route. The math didn't add up, and it didn't account for the fact that we would also need to descend the same route.

It didn't come even close to fitting into my plan to live to old age, the 100-year plan.

I lay back down, feeling deeply frustrated.

Another avalanche of rocks came down, this time larger than the last. I again looked at the thermometer on my watch. It now read 14 degrees Celsius.

Ian and I were rattled, and we ran through the different scenarios. As we picked apart the conditions and timing, it became clear that we needed to go back down to base camp and hope the weather cooled down. In our chosen style of climbing, our margin of safety was already small, and continuing to climb would subject us to a far greater chance of death than either of us was willing to take. It was simply too hot. When the temperatures cooled in the evening, we would head down.

Sitting back on my ledge, I once again looked at the winding West Ridge beneath us. It was no longer just the way that we had come but also the path we would take in retreat. It was the same terrain I had been looking at an hour earlier, but now it looked different. Now it represented the 6,000 feet of the route we had climbed and bailed. Progress, seemingly, to nowhere.

I thought back to other times I had looked down a route like this. Staring down the sheer northeast buttress of Mount Laurens in Alaska, or the southeast wall of Link Sar in Pakistan. They were times that, due to conditions, weather, equipment failure, or technical challenge, I had been forced to retreat. They were times when I had reached an often hard-to-define line that I dared not cross for fear of not returning. Yet,

I had learned from each of these decisions and subsequently survived to continue to pursue the practice of alpinism. Eventually, I had always come back stronger and better.

I was also grateful for other memories, times in which my partners and I had decided to push forward into the unknown of a steep wall, one pitch at a time. Reaching for one more handhold or seeking the next piece of protection that would unlock the climbing above. They were times when we had defined for ourselves the vague difference between danger and fear—the former to be avoided, the latter to be explored and, if possible, set aside.

As I looked down the West Ridge of Chogori, I knew that despite the frustration I felt, this was another lesson in humility that I would process in time and reflect upon for the rest of my life.

We tend to think of expeditions as times of action, but I have found this to be a misconception. Alpine climbing in the big mountains of the world requires long periods of rest and waiting for the right climbing conditions. These considerable moments of pause have consistently been a boon in my life, offering me time to reflect and gather my thoughts, far away from the churning of the world below.

Oftentimes, I set myself tasks for this downtime. Generally, these are things I would like to learn or decisions I would like to make, tasks that require a large amount of mental space and time to digest, like getting married, buying a house, or making career pivots.

During my 2021 expedition to the high Karakoram, I set myself the goal of constructing the bulk of this manuscript. When storms raged or my body was hammered from days on the mountain, I sat in my tent, sipping tea, and revisited the more than 30 expeditions I had undertaken, in an effort to describe how I fell in love with the practice of climbing and how it, alongside the amazing community of folks who participate in it, has taught me far more than I could have ever expected.

In his book *The Innovators*, about the creation of modern computing, Walter Isaacson wrote that progress "usually comes not from an individual brainstorm but from a collaboratively woven tapestry of creativity." I feel that alpinism, or mountain climbing, is another such tapestry, composed of lessons gathered by generations of people who have dedicated their lives to ascending mountains.

I have been fortunate to be a part of a generation of mountain climbers who have had the opportunity to accomplish some amazing things. Many of these folks are still with us, but a number are not. Some of these are people I might consider better suited to have written this story, if not for their loss while attempting to discover the cutting edge of what it means to be a climber and a human. During the past decade, I have lost many partners and kindred souls—people who defined our generation by pouring their hearts into this practice. In many ways, I feel that I am writing this book because I am one of my generation of alpinists in the United States left to tell this tale. It's a role I take on with a strong sense of honor, responsibility, and sadness; this story is a tribute to those whom we have lost to this practice.

Writing this in my mid-30s, I still have many years of learning ahead of me. Climbing is a practice that defines who I am and that I will continue until the end of my life—hopefully as an old man. This book simply stands as a signpost along the way.

1

Vitalogy

I leaned back from the belay as the storm bashed against the pillar of rock and ice projecting from the south face of Mount Bradley in Alaska. Only a few days before, under clear skies, my partner Mark and I had looked up at the feature from the glacier below. We'd discussed what it would feel like to be climbing in that position with thousands of feet of exposure beneath our feet. We imagined the exhilaration of progress on the steep terrain. Now, hanging from our belay, I shrugged deeper into my jackets as the wind wailed around our exposed position. It brought a barrage of snow in its swirling gusts. We couldn't see the glacier below. Tired, cold, and hungry after a long day of climbing, we needed shelter from the storm. We needed a place to regroup, a bivouac where we could stop, set up the tent, and rest.

Mark recalled seeing a small ledge out to the right while following the pitch below. I fixed the ropes to the anchor and he rappelled. A few minutes later, I heard him shout back up through the storm, "We're psyched! Get down here!"

The granite ledge was barely large enough for the two of us to lay side by side. We cleared it off and constructed our tent. The corner of our small nylon shelter hung precariously over the edge, but it didn't matter. We dove in. Carefully avoiding the side that was hanging over the void, we took deep breaths of still air and settled down, safe within the tent. The storm still raged outside, but we had the moment of reprieve that we needed. I felt myself relax as I took a deep breath—*finally*, I thought, *we can regroup*.

We each carried a 35-liter backpack and inside the tent we unpacked them, digging out the supplies that would allow us to survive the night. We had a stove, a now half-empty can of gas, a medical kit, sleeping pads, two small sleeping bags, and some food that we assembled into a small pile: a few energy bars and a single freeze-dried meal. It was all the supplies we had left.

Our plan had been to spend one night on the wall. This was our third, with over 3,000 feet below us and 1,000 feet of climbing still above. We had seriously misjudged the route, but despite the storm and our meager rations, we kept going.

"I think we're going to need most of this for tomorrow," Mark said quietly. We started repacking everything other than the freeze-dried food into a stuff sack. I looked at the nutritional information—we'd be getting less than 400 calories each.

As we sat, passing the bag of rehydrated meal back and forth, we didn't discuss going down. Later, curled up in my sleeping bag, I felt the tent fabric rub cold against my face and wondered if we should—or, with our equipment, if we could. But even as snow pounded the outside of the tent, I saw no viable reason to retreat, other than hunger. I closed my eyes and thought back to years of reading climbing literature. I was sure that this was it. We were doing it. The discomfort, the feeling of approaching a ragged edge—this is what we wanted.

Mark Allen and I had met eight years before. I was in high school and Mark was a greenhorn climbing guide, engaged in the training necessary to become fully certified. I had discovered climbing as a high schooler living in North Seattle. My parents were always supportive of my pursuits, but my enthusiasm for the vertical caused them to fear for my life. They had signed me up for a mountaineering course so I could learn proper safety measures, and Mark was the instructor. At the end of the course, he invited me to get in touch if I was ever in his hometown of Mazama, on the eastern slope of Washington's North Cascade Mountains. A few weeks later, I banged on his door. I was 16 and all I wanted to do was continue to learn about climbing. Mark needed a partner for local projects. I was excited to join. Under his tutelage, I ascended my first vertical frozen waterfalls, made my first turns in the deep backcountry, and consumed some of my first beers. As we climbed, I experienced a sense of freedom and challenge that was unlike anything else in my life; it took me away from the day-to-day drudgery of being a teenager and forced me to be responsible for my decisions. And the consequences were far more serious than a bad grade or being pulled from a soccer field—I was making decisions that kept me alive. It made the world around me feel more real: beautiful, dangerous, and full of opportunity.

It was during this time that Mark, while we were driving in his truck to a crag, handed me a copy of Mark Twight's book *Extreme Alpinism: Climbing Light, Fast, and High.*

Twight was part of the climbing generation just before my own, and—through his adventures and his words—he extolled their ethos. His crew of climbers, mostly men, saw alpinism as an elite practice. For them to be at the cutting edge was to trim away anything else. No extra weight, no extra emotion, no ties to the ground. The best climbing was a face-off between man and mountain on the simplest terms.

This was part of a rebellion against the climbing style pioneered decades before, when ropes were slowly fixed up mountains, over a period of months, oftentimes up the easiest routes. Large teams would work together to establish a lifeline—an umbilical cord of nylon rope—setting up and stocking camps as they went. They sieged the mountain until it submitted. It was in this way that many of the first ascents of the 1950s and 1960s were made. These tactics had also seen a resurgence of commercial expeditions to peaks like Mount Everest, where a massive price tag could be attached to this simplified path to the summit. Twight and his partners were having none of it, embracing and advancing the practice of alpinism instead.

Following in the footsteps of climbers like the Polish mountaineer Voytek Kurtyka, the alpinists rejected the concept of fixed ropes and stocked camps. They chose instead to bring only what they could carry on their backs and the length of rope tied between them. Together, they took it a step further, forgoing sleep and any equipment that wasn't absolutely necessary until they stepped into a house of pain, chained together searching for that truth ascribed to German philosopher Nietzsche as "beyond good and evil." They lived by the principle that talk without action is nothing, as they pushed forward in their effort to become the Übermensch, or superior man, through the practice of alpinism.

In *Extreme Alpinism*, Twight describes alpine climbing in muscular and aggressive language. There were images of him and his partners hanging by the tips of their ice tools on severe pitches of rock on huge mountains. I learned that this was called mixed climbing, and the images were my first exposure to what was truly possible in the high hills of the world. I didn't have any sense of the lands through which Twight and his partners had traveled; I saw only the massive landscape of mountains—places where these men were filling in the undrawn details of the atlas, one stroke at a time. Within that book I saw a path forward that piqued my curiosity. It was a path on which I could test myself against the world's most intimidating features.

Now eight years later, in 2010, I hoped to taste what it meant to sit on the bleeding edge of lightweight technical alpinism—in Alaska. I put the expenses on a credit card, texted my parents goodbye, turned off my phone, and flew north, leaving everything behind. I forgot about the woman I was dating and my job in Yosemite. I was in the moment to either succeed or be maimed. I was there to take on the mountains, to see if I withstood the test.

For Mark and me, this trip to the Great Gorge of the Ruth marked the first time we had tied in together in six years, but we picked right back up. We fell back into an easy flow of congenial banter as we packed and flew onto the glacier. In many ways it was the same, but the difference was that now we were climbing as equals, bringing our own specific skills to the endeavor. Mark, now a certified IFMGA Mountain Guide, had accrued an immense skill set for managing the mountains. I had been focused on climbing technical routes, having made my first expeditions to the world's larger ranges. I had found success on a big, new mixed route in the Pamirs of Kyrgyzstan and opened a new route on a granite wall in Chilean Patagonia, but I had yet to feel the edge I read about in climbing literature. I yearned for it.

▲

"**JUST RIGHT OF** the horizon line, ending below the tower," I told Mark, passing him our binoculars and pointing out a spot high on the east face of Mount Bradley where a thin line of ice slithered upward on the largest part of the wall. We willfully overlooked the sheer granite faces both above and below the line of ice.

Looking up at the route, I compared it to El Capitan in Yosemite—the face on Bradley was only a little taller and not nearly as steep. I had been climbing El Cap in well under 24 hours. We convinced ourselves that the route would only take a day and a half.

This is the warm-up, it won't be that big of a deal.

After one false start, we launched on April 2 with supplies for 36 hours. We felt strong, we were excited, and we were ready to test ourselves on the mountain.

The climbing started up a steepening, sickle-shaped snow gully to a deep cave. Seeking cold nighttime temperatures, we started climbing in the late afternoon. As I pulled out of the roof of the cave onto a continuously steep granite shield, the sun sank and the range exploded with color, the horizon awash with oranges and reds that reflected off the tremendous walls surrounding us. Three more pitches of torquing and hooking while placing pitons and cams in solid gray rock passed in the evening light, after which I turned on my head torch and handed off the lead to Mark.

On smooth rock, he changed out of his crampons and into rock shoes, mid-lead. Under the beams of our lights, the exposure below us disappeared. We felt no fatigue. We were loaded with anticipation and emotion. We were having fun.

As the sun rose, we pulled through snow onto the top of a steep prow. In the warming air of the clear morning, we set up our tent to sit out the heat of the day, sleeping and eating. Unconcerned that we still had over two-thirds of the wall above us, we were immersed in the flow of the experience. We were managing risks and moving well together; my mind was absent of anything besides the climbing. We were also delighted when we found a nearly flat spot beneath an outcropping of rock on which to bivouac. When we felt the temperature starting to cool, we started out again.

Just above us lay the thin ice ribbon. It appeared to be thick 200 feet up but petered out into the rocks above the snow ledge on which we had situated our belay. I hooked on smooth granite and gently tapped my tools into verglas while searching for security, which remained elusive. It was steep, pushing my weight onto my hands. As I tied off one of my shortest ice screws, I visualized the satisfaction of having finished the pitch and let it draw me upward. Eventually, I reached thicker ice and then the end of the rope. I built a belay and Mark climbed up to join me. Above us, thick water ice was nestled into a chimney. As the sun once again set, Mark took over the lead, swinging and kicking methodically.

Establishing a second bivy at sunrise, we expected to traverse to the right into easy terrain. An extra night out was of no concern. We had read countless stories of climbers spending an extra night on the hill; we were still feeling strong.

We woke to lenticular clouds on the horizon. Their uniform lens shape signals incoming wind and moisture. "Our window is closing," Mark muttered, speaking as much to himself as to me. We packed quickly and continued up a steep, blocky mixed ridge.

The first storm hit. The intended easier terrain to our right ran with heavy spindrift avalanches. We could hear the snow hissing down the concavities in the wall. We were forced to aim for protrusions from the wall and found ourselves at the base of a 1,000-foot tower of rock. In clear weather, the climbing on it would have been fantastic—it was steep and well protected—but the storm raging around us made every pitch feel desperate. We pushed through seven pitches of sustained climbing, torquing our ice picks in cracks and reaching above our heads, groping for hooks on the granite. We climbed until we were spent, then fixed our line and rappelled down to the bivy ledge Mark had spied, 200 feet below us.

Sleep was fitful. Our bodies were losing the edge we had felt so acutely. With our energy stores running low, we were leaning harder into adrenaline and instinct.

But even as we flirted with the murky line between survival and exploration, I was not afraid of dying. I recognized the seriousness of the situation, but as I listened to the snow blowing by, I felt that I was keeping my hand steady as I stared into the void. It didn't bother me. I was confident I would be able to step back from the edge.

▲

THIS IS WHAT *you came for, this is what you yearn for, this is everything you want.*

The next morning, the weather cleared around us as we climbed steep, exposed snow slopes and spines, clawing slowly up the tower through fresh snow over weathered granite.

At 4:00 p.m., after a punishingly endless period of time, which our clocks showed as only 67 hours, we made the final steps to the summit of Mount Bradley. The sun was still high; we reached our arms in the air while hollering at the horizon. It was a long way down—and the second half of a climb, the descent, is often more dangerous than the first—but from that moment on, our vector would be pointed toward the safety of camp rather than away from it.

We shared the final half of an energy bar before starting down Mount Bradley's west ridge. In front of us stood the magnificent pyramidal east face of Mount Huntington, with slashes of steep rock ribs running diagonally down its wall like a swipe from the talons of some mythical beast. It quickly disappeared as a second storm closed in, obscuring our descent. We had read that reaching the glacier below was easy, but as we lost visibility and the snow loaded the slopes beneath us, we were forced onto steeper terrain, now descending the opposite side of the peak from the one we had climbed. We lost track of scale as we downclimbed and rappelled 2,500 feet of unknown terrain.

We didn't converse much as we stayed concentrated on the task, our focus refined by the intensity of the situation. Rock anchors, V-threads, and a severely overhanging rappel over a final gaping crevasse passed as the sun set and the storm intensified. Finally, we were able to walk—yet we were still not safe. We were on the far side of the peak from camp, surrounded by seracs and snow-loaded slopes that we could not see so much as hear as they released and slid down the mountain. The falling snow settled onto their inclines, increasing the avalanche potential above us.

Seven hours after summiting, we hurried down the glacier and bivied beneath a rock overhang at the base of one of the steep, glacially carved walls. It was our third unplanned bivy. The storm lasted all day, pinning us down. It brought 12 inches of new snow and waist-deep drifts as we sat in our tent, hungry, exhausted, trying to stay dry. We considered our options. We had approximately four miles of complex glacier terrain—over a pass and back into the Ruth Gorge—to base camp. I looked out of the tent to the storm outside. Quickly zipping the tent again, I turned to Mark, who was poring over maps.

"We're not going anywhere in these conditions," I submitted. We would have to wait.

We lost track of time sitting in the small tent waiting for the storm to pass. We dozed. The sun came up, but the storm raged on. "I wonder if we can eat our gloves," Mark debated with himself, aloud. We dozed again. As morning shifted into afternoon, I was awakened from more napping by a sizable avalanche, caused by direct sunlight on the slope above, as it poured over the rim of our rock awning. The edge of the avalanche pummeled our tent, making us panic, but it indicated that finally the weather was clearing. It was time to leave.

As we slogged across the glacier, my body hurt and my stomach growled. We had been without food for nearly 30 hours. I forced myself to focus on the final destination of base camp as we struggled along the glacier through waist-deep snow. The walls around us rose to an overwhelmingly large scale as they peeked in and out of the clouds. Most of them were unclimbed. We kept our eyes cast down, unable to push the trail forward more than 300 feet at a time. We traded leads, over and over again. Slowly we proceeded to the top of the pass that sits between Mount Dickey and Mount Bradley.

At the top of the pass, we looked down onto the familiar expanse of the Ruth Glacier and dared to feel safe. Then, as the sun set, a third storm blew in. Once again, our visibility was reduced to the clouds and swirling snow immediately in front of us. We donned our headlamps, but their light reflected off the snow and moisture, further reducing our ability to see where we were going. We knew we were close, but we didn't know where exactly to go.

The final two miles back to camp dragged on as we slogged. When we sensed we were getting close, we started to zigzag across the glacier, searching for our camp. Darkness caught us out for another night and combined with the clouds to make our search slow and tedious. I focused all my energy away from fatigue and hunger, but I was sluggish and frustrated as I searched for any changes in the snow's surface that would indicate camp—or danger. Finally, we came across a strange rib in the snow that extended beyond our small field of vision. We followed it for 300 feet to where we found our camp. It was snowed under, and a fan had formed in its wind shadow, creating the rib that had guided us back, saving us from another hungry night out.

2

Alpinist of the Year, in New Zealand

[JUNE 2011]

I sipped black coffee from a paper cup while looking out the small, oval-shaped window of the Air New Zealand 747. The Pacific Ocean passed by, 30,000 feet below. Its azure-blue hue, partially obscured by clouds, provided an open palette for reflection. Fourteen hours on an airplane was a welcome pause from what felt like a life of constant movement.

It had been just over a year since Mark and I had completed the first ascent of the route we named *Vitalogy* on the south face of Mount Bradley in Alaska. In those months, my climbing career had turned a corner. After five expeditions to the world's high mountains, I signed a series of small contracts for sponsorship. I then proceeded to go on more expeditions.

I also landed a job on a geophysics team searching for minerals in far-flung corners of the world. It was a major upgrade from what I had earned working for climbing shops and on the Yosemite Search and Rescue team. I walked away from my first geology contract with enough money to start a small investment account, cover the costs of my next expedition, and buy myself a new pair of jeans. I felt powerful. I no longer felt like I was living on the edge of poverty. It gave me a sense of security and independence that I had never before experienced.

I had also been climbing. A lot. From frozen pillars of ice in Montana to vertical walls in the mountains of Colorado and Washington, I was putting in my time and I was getting better.

I was traveling so frequently that there was no reason to rent an apartment, and my constant focus on climbing had meant that multiple women deemed me "undatable," but that didn't matter to me. I was climbing nearly full-time and I was financially solvent. To me, it all looked like success. Having just returned from another series of trips to Alaska, and wearing those new jeans, I was on an airplane headed to New Zealand to receive the award for 2010 Kiwi Alpinist of the Year.

To many, my New Zealand background came as a surprise. Other than a few odd pronunciations and a bit of Kiwi vernacular, I presented as American. And, in fact, I was a full-blooded Yankee but for a quirk of my personal history.

I was born in New Zealand on January 30, 1986. My parents had recently moved from the flatlands of Kansas to the capital city of Wellington and, subsequently, I was born a dual citizen. My earliest memories are of remote beaches and deep forests from road trips around the rugged South Island with my parents—and, eventually, my younger sister, Greer. New Zealand was a delightful place of mystery and wonder, where folks young and old were encouraged to explore, where getting dirty was acceptable, and where adventure and discovery were a strong part of the culture.

It was during this time that I had my first experience in the mountains. As a family, we took a flight onto Fox Glacier, a massive glacial system on the west coast of the South Island. The flight was short and affordable, standard tourist fare. We stepped out from the small helicopter to views across the expanse of ice, with the Tasman Sea to the west and the precipitous peaks of the Southern Alps to the east. When I look at the photos of us standing outside the helicopter, our faces reflect a sense of awe for the stunning landscape. And while I don't personally remember details of the trip, I am confident that it burrowed into my subconscious, as it was a place that I would return 15 years later, ice tools in hand.

By 1989, I was three years old and getting ready to start school. My folks decided they had spent enough time far away from family, so Dad accepted a job in the growing tech sector in Seattle, nestled between the Salish Sea and the Cascade Range. It was here that I grew up and had many of my first formative mountain experiences, but family stories about the peaks of New Zealand were always in the back of my mind.

We moved to Edmonds, a small town north of Seattle. It was a sleepy community situated on the edge of the calm sea, best known as the ferry departure point used to reach the Olympic Peninsula.

Growing up in the soft confines of middle-class America, I participated in sports but never found myself deeply invested. To my young mind, soccer matches and Frisbee games were social affairs and the outcomes didn't matter. Later in my teens, when I tried to build a competitive edge, I didn't know how. It blended with a potent dose of hormones, resulting in frustration but few wins.

Looking back now, I realize I was searching for an activity and an environment in which I could be inspired and find meaning. I was looking for a place I could define a direction for myself, where I could define my limits and learn how to step beyond them. Eventually, I found it in the mountains.

It started with backcountry skiing along the crest of ridges above Washington's Stevens Pass ski area. As friends and I clawed our way across the ridges, I found a simple joy in kicking steps along ribs of snow. As we went along, I peered down gullies that fell away beneath my feet. Those that were too steep for me to ski made the pit of my stomach ache. It was an uncomfortable yet not entirely bad feeling.

My curiosity quickly escalated to climbing and skiing volcanoes. Some of my father's work colleagues climbed, and he asked them to take me under their wing. Together we climbed Mount Adams, with its 6,000 feet of vertical relief, and Glacier Peak, situated far from any road, deep in the Cascades. They were ascents that took days rather than hours and required a much larger pack.

My memories of those early climbs are rife with challenge and discomfort. I look back on them fondly, but I don't remember enjoying them. I failed to eat enough food or put on sunscreen, ending up exhausted and badly sunburned. Nor was the skiing particularly good. I remember the uneven, partially melted surface threatened to loosen my molars as I skittered over it.

Given those initial experiences, it's a curiosity that I found myself drawn back to the mountains. Maybe it was a sense that I could have done better. Or maybe it was just so unlike anything I had ever experienced in my comfortable suburban American life that I needed another sampling.

Whatever it was, I started returning to the mountains frequently. Soon my time at home was spent reading the climber's bible: *Mountaineering: The Freedom of the Hills*, a literal textbook on mountaineering. I read it cover to cover, following its every instruction—even when it told me I needed to be able to tie knots in a cold shower in the dark, which I took literally.

My parents encouraged me to try but also asked me to be careful. It was this encouragement that landed me in that fateful course with Mark Allen and exposed me to a version of alpinism far beyond my scampering around on the hills outside of Seattle.

As a privileged white kid growing up in the suburbs, it had been easy to avoid pain or severe challenge. I knew I wanted something outside of the bounds of the small, safe town I lived in, even though I couldn't have articulated it at the time. The mountains offered it to me. It was something deep and complex that I had never experienced before.

It was more than the muscular strain of pulling myself up steep terrain. It was something closer to blood in my mouth after a fight that I have never experienced. I liked the taste. It was tickling a dark corner of my heart that, up until that point, I didn't know existed. It was a part of me I wanted to get to know better.

I recall Mark and me climbing ice flows that had formed on a road-cut below the Liberty Bell Group near Mazama. I had just purchased my first pair of ice tools from a shop where I had convinced the manager to give me a few hours of work between classes. Every dime I made was spent on gear, including the bright orange ice tools with RAGE scrawled down the side.

We started on the thick flows that could handle our ice tools as we swung repeatedly until we had the perfect stick. As the day wore on, we started trying to piece together blobs of ice that didn't connect. They forced us to swing carefully, lest we destroy the thin ice. I held my breath as I gently weighted each placement, sure that the pick would tear away from its shallow hold in the thin veneer, but it never did.

We climbed with a rope above us and a tight belay at our waist. A fall would have been safe. But I let myself imagine this kind of terrain in the mountains, with the rope dangling beneath me, only available to catch me after many feet of falling. I flexed my hands, feeling the moisture on my palms as I wondered if it was really something I wanted to pursue. Despite the intimidation, I continued to take small steps toward bigger, more technical routes.

The different types of alpine climbing felt nearly limitless and, as winter turned to summer, I started to look toward the rock walls of the Cascade Range. If I was to become competent in the mountains, I would need to understand how to climb any piece of terrain I encountered, whether frozen flows of ice or sheer rock walls devoid of snow.

Mount Garfield in the central Cascades would be a wholly insignificant peak, were it not home to a massive, easy-to-access rock climb. Einar, a climber from North Seattle, and I cast off up its near-endless 2,300 feet of smooth slab. Most of the climbing was moderate, and the pitches fell away beneath us as we ascended. Above us the final headwall reared up like a wave, standing vertical before breaking.

The hardest pitches of the route were on that headwall. As I stepped out onto them in the lead, I was aware that they were at the very limit of my abilities. I focused, holding my body tight as I moved from hold to hold up the vertical granite. The world fell away. I took deep breaths. The exposure disappeared. I surrendered to a simple meditation of movement. Reaching the anchor, I was astonished to find that the pitch had felt neither challenging nor stressful; it had simply felt good.

I didn't have a particularly refined idea of what I wanted to climb, or how I wanted to do it, but I had been told the mountains of New Zealand were the ultimate training ground for the biggest and baddest peaks on the planet. When I graduated from high school in 2004, I therefore pointed my sights at the South Island and the spine that ran its length: the Southern Alps. I planned to attend the University of Otago in Dunedin on the southeastern coast, but more importantly, I wanted to cut my teeth on the island's high and heavily glaciated peaks.

Just before the New Year's Eve that was to kick off the year 2005, I flew to Christchurch with two duffel bags of climbing equipment, a wallet full of savings from summer jobs building trails, and a level of enthusiasm available only to a young person on their first big adventure. I drove with a new climbing partner, Tom, to the thin strip of western coastline smashed between the wilds of the Tasman Strait and the Southern Alps that rise directly off the beach. The powerful low-pressure systems that circulate clockwise around Antarctica, the same that make the famous storms of Patagonia, crash into this steep wall of terra firma. There, they transition into ferocious weather, coating the mountains with the snow and ice that craft the massive glaciers and steep, ice-laden walls of the main divide of New Zealand's biggest mountain range.

Along this rugged coastline is the small township of Fox Glacier, which I had visited with my parents so many years before. This time, when the helicopter landed, my attention was focused on the steep lines of snow and ice threading their way up to the high summits that pushed upward so dramatically from the rolling ocean of ice.

The mountains of New Zealand are dotted with huts—small refuges built and maintained by the New Zealand Alpine Club. Made from metal and wood, tucked in among the high-alpine environment, they are oftentimes mounted onto spines of rock protruding above turbulent rivers of ice. Some can be reached by walking, for others the only feasible approach is to hire a helicopter for the short flight to a nearby landing zone.

Climbers can choose a hut, fly in, and use it as a sort of base camp from which they can attempt the mountains above. When their supplies run out, or the mountains become overwhelming, they can use the radio mounted inside the hut's door to call town and request a ride back to the safety of the valley below.

I spent my summer popping in and out of these high alpine huts, and I became attuned to the hills above them. I learned how to read the jumbles of glacial ice while approaching walls and how to pivot my mind quickly to the routes themselves, as we followed winding paths of ice-laden corners up steep faces leading to jagged and distinct summits.

The Unwin hut is a larger facility situated just down the road from Mount Cook Village. For two months, it was my home base from which I walked or flew into the clutch of peaks around Mount Cook. From the front of the hut, I could see three of the biggest and steepest faces in the range—the south faces of Hicks, Sefton, and Cook. Climbing these became my goal.

New Zealand has a deep tradition of alpinism. Climbers who trained on the peaks of that small island nation have taken their skills to the great ranges of the Himalaya, Karakoram, Andes, and Alaska, where they put up some of the most formidable routes in the world. And unlike climbers in the United States, where climbing is countercultural, climbers in New Zealand have been celebrated by the nation. Sir Edmund Hillary, who made the first ascent of Everest in 1953 alongside Sherpa Tenzing Norgay, is on the county's five-dollar note.

The pioneering Kiwi climbers hold a high level of respect among their contemporary countrymen. Their names are revered and written next to some of the greatest ascents of their generations. As I pawed through the guidebook to the Southern Alps, I saw them—Whimp, Denz, Deavoll—next to the most demanding routes. I followed the lines drawn in the guide as they snaked their way up improbably steep terrain. I imagined joining their ranks, pushing into the unknown on the big hills of the world. I wondered what it would feel like to see the terrain they had seen.

Over the next three years, I studied geology and glaciers at the University of Otago, but all my free time was spent pursuing my forebearers' footsteps through those mountains, where I learned more about clinging to their steepest aspects, one climb at a time.

On the south face of Mount Cook, I watched my partner, a Brit named Mark Kendrick, steadily progress up the vertical ice of the route's steepest pitch. To his right, a massive glacial serac hung over the void, its icy-gray tint punctuated by cracks in the ice along its side; tons of ice ready to crash thousands of feet to the glacier below. As we climbed the final pitches before the route rolled over into a moderate ridgeline, I was overwhelmed with exhaustion. When we reached the summit ridge, I told Mark that I needed to go down. I was sure that if I went any higher, I would perish. Mark, having noticed that I had neglected to eat all day, made me consume a whole salami and told me to wait 20 minutes.

Once the time had passed and my body had started to metabolize the meat stick, I felt better. Mark's actions made me realize what I was capable of as a climber, particularly if I fueled myself properly. We charged to the summit.

The south face of Sefton took Andrew Rennie, Jon Loeffler, and me 26 hours to climb. Deep winter snows forced us to swim through any low-angle terrain; when we finally reached the face's steep upper headwall, the near-vertical ice felt easy. On the descent back to our bivy below the face, I hallucinated due to exhaustion and Jon suffered bad frostbite on his toes. As I thawed them out of his boots, it was a first taste of the harsh reality of the mountains.

Later that year, on the south face of Mount Hicks, again with Mark Kendrick, now a regular climbing partner, I felt my training come together. The incredibly steep ice plastered to the wall fell away beneath our tools, one pitch at a time. At a junction between two routes, we opted toward the steeper, linking together two of the steepest routes on the wall. As we popped our heads over the summit, we were hit by a massive storm pouring into the range. In our effort to survive the spindrift avalanches, we left most of our equipment on the mountain but came away unharmed.

As I learned how to identify climbable terrain, I started exploring new territory, which led to opening new routes on the lesser peaks of the range. Encouraged by the adventures of generations before us, my partners and I had a curiosity that drove us to explore unknown contours and push into unclimbed pitches of mixed rock and ice. It stoked intimidation and no small amount of fear. At the same time, the payoff of standing on top of a route that had never been climbed felt incredible. It was another small step into a realm in which I faced off against some of nature's most severe features, with only the wits and experience I shared with my partners to guide our way forward.

This trajectory would lead me over the next three years to make my first forays into the big mountains—chasing new lines of unclimbed terrain in the Pamirs, the Alaska Range, and the Andes, eventually leading me to that flight headed back to New Zealand. I was 25, the same age as my father when he and my mother moved to New Zealand from Kansas.

I arrived in Auckland and immediately started a slideshow tour, performing talks for the various sections of the New Zealand Alpine Club. When I showed up at these events—held in pubs, with their ubiquitous booths, high tables, and smell of beer—the New Zealand climbing community welcomed me back with open arms.

Feeling that I was a novelty and needed to explain my lack of a Kiwi accent, I started with my origin story. I went on to tell the story of my first expedition to Alaska, where Ian Nicholson, Ryan O'Connell, and I had flown into the Kichatna Spires, staring out the window at the approaching peaks, bewildered by the size of their vertical granite walls. Over the next few weeks, we climbed nearly 5,000 feet of new terrain but never got near any summits. Instead, we were turned back by storms and hard climbing.

I continued with my story of sneaking over the Tajik border in a military truck with Paul Hersey and Yewjin Tan to access the remote Pamir Alai mountains of southwest Kyrgyzstan. Intermittent storms kept us in base camp until Yewjin and I decided to take nearly nothing on a 4,500-foot mixed wall. Traveling without a tent felt so freeing— until our third bivy, where we realized with a sickening reality that our single rope and meager rack meant we had no option other than to make it to the top.

Next, I took the audience down to Chilean Patagonia, again with Ian Nicholson, where we sat in the forests of the Torres del Paine during weeks of rain. We drank wine with the Russians until an 18-hour window of clear weather allowed us to sprint for a peak called Los Gemelos, The Twins. Chasing splitter cracks, we ran up a new route. We employed tactics learned on the big walls of Yosemite—short-fixing and guerrilla aid. As we headed upward, the dark of a storm set in. The photo of us on top, after thrutching up a wide crack to reach the summit, showed a wildness of exhilaration and exhaustion in our eyes. I then shared videos from Mount Bradley and told the story of our climb of *Vitalogy* and the subsequent descent—when we ended up in a snowstorm on the wrong side of the mountain.

The stories I told left out the hours of manual labor and working at grocery stores to pay for the expeditions, or how I didn't have a home outside of a storage unit and the promise of a hot meal and clean bed at my folks' house. Instead, they focused on the three years of concentrated climbing I'd done since graduating from university. They also related how climbing in New Zealand had given me the tools I needed to climb in the big mountains of the world. The old-timers in the crowd sat back, sipping their beers and beaming with pride for their home mountains. I watched inspiration infect the youngsters as they leaned in, as I would have done only a few short years before. It felt like I had made a name for myself as a climber—and, according to my plans, I was only just getting started.

The official ceremony for the national award was held in Christchurch. I told my stories to a crowd of 40 people as they sat in the poorly lit Irish pub. They once again quietly sipped beers as I spun now well-practiced yarns about the mountains that were shaping me as a climber. Once finished, I was handed the large wooden statue depicting a climber with his axe in hand and a coil of rope over his shoulder. Each year it was passed to the recipient of the award; this year it was mine to hold. Small bronze plaques on the trophy listed the names of past recipients, many of whom were sitting in front of me. A fresh plaque carried my name.

Most of the audience departed, but a small group of us stayed in a booth at the back of the bar late into the night. As we sat hunched over our refills, I peered at the dimly lit faces around me as they told stories about far-off peaks. These were faces etched with the creases of years spent close to the sun in rarefied air. Having already talked onstage for most of the evening, I listened to my alpine climbing heroes telling tales of clinging to the biggest mountains in the world. Through the haze of a few pints, I was amazed that these folks had now become my peers. Slowly, I was becoming a notable member of this community. My chest tightened in pride at the realization.

Following the award ceremony, my heart was full and my ego was empowered. I had a few days off from presentations, so I headed back into the mountains of the South Island, eager for a taste of the terrain that had taught me so much of what I knew. I was staying with my good friends Paul and Shelley Hersey in Christchurch. Paul was a longtime climber and author with whom I had climbed both in New Zealand and Kyrgyzstan. I had also climbed with Shelley, his wife. They were the consummate climbing couple: Paul was a big, tough alpinist with a surfer's build and a strong chin, Shelley was an exceptionally strong woman whose smile widened when things got challenging.

"We spied an unclimbed ice route tucked into a remote valley south of Mount Cook," Paul told me. "Want to come along?"

I eagerly accepted.

Winter lay heavy on the valley, a thin coat of snow dusting the walls above us. Only the bottoms of the peaks were visible below the ceiling of storm clouds. It was cold and gloomy, perfect for ice climbing. As we walked, we chatted about mountains far afield, in the big ranges of the world. Paul and Shelley were headed to India to attempt an unclimbed peak; I had plans to go back to northeastern Africa to work another geology contract and then to Alaska to climb. But it was hard to pull myself away from the stunning scenery surrounding us. It was a landscape that I felt a deep affinity toward, both for time spent there and lessons learned.

That night we slept in a hut before heading up a side valley to the line of ice. Winding its way up into a gully for 500 feet to a snowfield below the ridgeline, it was not as steep as I had hoped. My ego, inflated by the recent award ceremony, wanted to make a daring first ascent, which that sliver of ice in front of us was definitely not. But I didn't share this with my partners as we racked up. It didn't matter. I was in the mountains with dear friends, traveling into unknown terrain. It would be fun.

Racked up and brimming with confidence, I didn't bother to tie in to the rope on the first pitch. Instead, I opted to free solo alongside Shelley as she led, taking photos as I went. I snapped images of her as she climbed. Through the viewfinder, I watched as she carefully swung her axes into the ice and kicked her crampons in with practiced efficiency. She was in her element.

I climbed to Shelley's belay and clipped in. Paul seconded and then carried on leading up the second pitch. He made easy progress up the blue and white ice, occasionally placing screws for protection. Soon he arrived at an ice cave in which he built a belay.

On this pitch, I opted to tie in to the rope.

"Mind if I go ahead and climb next?" I asked Shelley.

She smiled. "Of course!"

Calling "Climbing!" up to Paul, I unclipped from the belay and felt the rope come snug at my waist. I stepped left into the thickest part of the flow and started making quick progress up the ice.

I was just into a rhythm, enjoying the meditation of quick movement, when a rumble came from above and Paul yelled, "*Ice!*"

Pressing myself against the wall, I hoped whatever was falling would bounce over me—but as it started to pour over, I could immediately tell this was a significant avalanche of ice and snow. Large chunks struck my helmet, knocking me off my stance. The barrage continued as I tumbled, hitting me hard on the leg and then my shoulder as I fell. I felt the rope stretch and eventually stop my fall. I was left hanging in the midst of falling ice, with no way to protect or shield myself.

After what felt like an eternity, the avalanche slowed and then stopped. Hanging on the end of the rope, suspended over the first pitch of the climb, I took two deep breaths and called up to my partners that I was conscious. Looking at the ground below, I could see that my decision to tie in had likely saved my life.

Paul and Shelley were both yelling. Paul had taken a glancing blow from the avalanche while Shelley had been safely tucked into her belay stance. I yelled again that I was conscious but that I thought I was hurt. Acute pain was starting to build in my shoulder and leg, and I could feel blood trickling down from my scalp.

They lowered me to the ground, where I untied and scuttled across the snow to a spot safe from any more falling debris. Sitting in the snow, I looked myself over. As adrenaline started to wash out of my system, I could feel that my right leg was exceptionally painful and my shoulder was nonfunctional. The foam of my helmet was split in two, deformed and cracked from the force of impact. A large laceration on my scalp was bleeding down my face; blood dripped off my eyebrow into the snow, melting it into water that then refroze, leaving red dots in the white. I wondered what had happened and what we would do next.

Paul and Shelley rappelled down. They quickly made their way over to me, clearly concerned with what they might find. I told them I was hurt but felt stable as they made their own assessment, checking my body for more injuries and making a plan. Paul was bleeding from his hands, having been hit while bare-handed. He looked to the sky, which was still a brooding overcast. A rescue operation would be long and arduous due to the poor flying conditions.

"Can you walk?" he asked.

"I think so," I replied, all confidence gone from my voice.

The approach from the hut to the climb had taken an hour. Hobbling down with the right side of my body crushed, it took three hours to get back. With each step, pain stabbed my leg, and my shoulder ached, but I knew stopping would only prolong the agony. I kept walking, leaning hard on a single trekking pole. Shelley and Paul carried my pack while helping in any way they could.

Arriving back at the hut, I lay down in one of the bunks while Paul and Shelley quietly discussed a plan. They decided that Paul would head down the valley to see if he could find someone with a four-wheel-drive truck that could make it up to the hut and give us a ride. As he headed out, Shelley started a brew on the stove.

As we sipped hot tea, the stress of the situation started to release. We laughed nervously at the absurdity of me having been injured after having just received the award for Alpinist of the Year. My shoulder stabbed with pain as I laughed, but it felt good to release a small amount of tension.

"The avalanche came from way up the climb," she said. "It had a lot of time to gain momentum before it hit you."

"Maybe a collapsing dagger of ice?" I asked. "Or maybe something had been blown off by the wind?"

These were rhetorical questions—we simply didn't know. We were just thankful that we were safe and, despite the pain in my shoulder and leg, I was stable. My scalp had stopped bleeding.

We didn't talk about what would have happened if I had not tied in.

Paul arrived back at the hut far sooner than expected. He had encountered some hunters driving their truck up the valley. They had immediately agreed to help.

As Shelley helped me into the back of their rig, two men in camo looked at me. I was bent over protecting my shoulder, and with dried blood streaked down my face and jacket. They quickly looked away.

"Without this ride, the walk would have been pretty unpleasant," I ventured, trying to make light of the situation. They were not amused.

Back at the trailhead, we thanked the hunters as they turned around and headed back into the valley. Climbing into Paul and Shelley's hatchback, we started the four-hour drive back to civilization and the hospital.

The nearest city large enough to have a hospital was Timaru, three hours south of Paul and Shelley's home in Christchurch. It was late when we arrived in town, exhausted and hungry. It had been a long day and we had not taken the time to eat. Knowing that it would be hard to get a meal in the hospital, I asked if we could stop for a burger. It was well past sunset when we pulled up to a fast-food place and, despite a protest from my partners, I crawled out of the car and hobbled inside.

Staggering out of the cool night air and into the fluorescent lights amid clean, plastic surfaces felt like entering another world, one to which I did not in this moment belong. The conversation in the restaurant quieted as all eyes drifted toward me. My right arm was tied up in a coil of rope, I was limping hard, and a stain of blood ran down my face and onto my bright green down jacket. I didn't care. Ignoring the attention, I walked across the restaurant to lean against the counter.

"Could I please have a burger and a water?" I asked, trying to act as if nothing was wrong. "Also, do you know how to get to the hospital?" Wide-eyed, the woman at the counter handed me the food and pointed me up the road.

At the hospital, I waited in the emergency department for an hour before seeing the doctor. X-rays showed that I had a broken bone in my leg and a shattered shoulder. Luckily, my head would be fine, as my helmet had taken the brunt of the impact. Wanting to monitor my condition, the doctors asked me to stay in the hospital, and asked Paul and Shelley to stay in the area. Despite my protests that they would be close enough at home, they got a hotel nearby.

The following morning, I was in the ICU listening to the beeps and whirs of the hospital room. I lay staring at the ceiling, frustrated by the injuries. I knew that all my progress, both as a climber and a professional, was now on hold. My whole life was on pause, and I suspected that it would be for weeks and months.

Sitting up, I looked at the other bed in the room, thankful it was empty. Winter sun shone through the window casting a golden light. I closed my eyes, thinking back to the accident, wondering what I could have done differently.

A light knock came at the door and a nurse came in with tea and breakfast. Seeing that I was awake, she smiled.

"Hi, hon. Is there anything I can get for you?"

I asked her if there was a phone that I could use to call my parents back in Seattle. A few minutes later she brought me a cordless phone. In my wallet, I had an international calling card. As I dialed the digits for the card, and then my parents' home phone, I dreaded telling them what had happened.

Dad picked up after two rings. It was a weekend early afternoon in Seattle, and he was delighted to hear my voice. He immediately called into another room, "Jane! Your boy is on the phone!"

He was excited to hear about the presentation tour but became quiet as I shared words that no parent wants to hear. "Hey, don't worry, I am fine, but I'm in the hospital." I tried to make my situation sound less severe than it was as I told him what had happened, but the simple facts of broken bones spoke for themselves. I was a mangled mess in an ICU on the far side of the globe.

Mom got on the phone. "Graham, honey, start from the beginning. What's going on?"

Once again I relayed the story. She quietly listened and then started asking about me getting home. I told her the doctor wanted to keep me in the hospital for a few days, after which I should be cleared to fly.

"We're here for anything you need," she said.

Then Dad got on the phone. "Get yourself home," he said. "We're so happy you're okay. We love you."

Two days later, I was released from the hospital, hobbling on a single crutch with instructions to find the best surgeon I could in the

Seattle area. My shoulder blade was crushed into eight fragments and the top of the joint had been pulverized. The doctor had told me the leg would heal just fine.

I had come back to New Zealand feeling in control of my life and on my way to becoming the climber I wanted to be. I was headed back in pieces, with nowhere to go other than my parents' house, with a deep sense of failure and a long road of recovery ahead of me.

3

A Slow Road to Recovery

I lay in bed with light from the street creeping through the window as the sounds of the city murmured through the walls. I was wide awake, trying to determine where I had gone wrong. The crashing of the ice rang through my head as the events in New Zealand ran through my mind over and over. I searched the experience for the mistake I had made—or the lesson to be learned. The ice had been cold, the climbing had been secure; there had been no warning signs, I didn't feel that we had made any bad decisions. I kept coming back to just being in the wrong place at the wrong time, stepping out into the gut of the gully at the precisely incorrect moment.

But this wasn't something I could learn from. It was just a simple demonstration that climbing is dangerous. And this, I did not like.

With nowhere else to go, I had crash-landed back at my parents' house—back and barely able to look after myself. They had welcomed me with open arms, never suggesting that I had made a mistake or trying to persuade me away from climbing. But it felt like failure.

Since I was unable to drive myself, Mom carted me between doctor appointments as they tried to solve the riddle of how to mend my shoulder blade that was now in eight pieces.

"You see in this image," said one doctor, pointing at a speck of white on the X-ray. "That's your coracoid process. It's separated from the rest of the scapula, and so is the acromion," pointing at another speck. "We need to get in there and plate it all back together."

Another doctor assured me that surgery was a bad option. "You're an athlete who has spent years developing your back and shoulder muscles," he said with a paternal tone. "Rather than cut through them, let's leave them be and let them hold everything in place while you heal."

The only consensus was that the top 10 percent of my glenoid—the dish of bone that makes up one side of the shoulder joint—was pulverized. "Nothing we can do about that," all the doctors seemed to say as they collectively tapped their pens against their clipboards.

In the end, I decided not to have an operation and to see if the puzzle pieces of broken bone would mend back together on their own. This meant two months of my shoulder being immobilized. My leg would be fine, the doctors assured me—just try not to limp too much.

I was unable to climb or go back to my geology work. Instead, I leaned into the small savings I had accumulated and my parents' insurance policy as I headed into an interminable cycle of physical therapy appointments and tried to solve the riddle of how to not let an accident like that happen again.

▲

I HAD BEEN living in massive expanses of natural space, where the sky ran out to distant horizons and the imprint of humanity was relegated to small areas cleared for tents, space where even the roads were forced to follow the contours of the terrain. The city was different;

natural spaces were small, engineered by planners to offset the asphalt and the buildings.

And there were so many people. After so much time in the mountains, I was unused to this much humanity in one place. I was just as uncomfortable seeing folks on the street, unbathed and asking for change, as I was seeing those employed in the local tech industry stepping out of exclusive restaurants in their sharp new clothes. Faced with this broad spectrum of human condition, I was unsure how I was meant to digest the inequity—and where I, a sometimes broke but socially advantaged mountain climber, stood within it.

In this urban space, the mountains felt very far away, and my search for a path forward threw my past into a new light. Reflecting on my climbing career up until this point, I had a hard time seeing success.

Before getting injured I had been extremely confident in my trajectory. I had been climbing with partners I trusted and adored on mountains that deeply inspired me. Now, all I was able to focus on were the mistakes and missteps. Where I had felt pride for the award in New Zealand and the ascent on Mount Bradley, I now saw a brazen ego and deadly climbing. I wondered if my pure drive to climb had led to more success than I could handle. Yet, I found myself wanting to get back to the mountains as quickly as possible. I still had so much that I wanted to accomplish.

▲

BEFORE HEADING ON that fateful trip to New Zealand, I had formed a partnership with a young climber named Hayden Kennedy. We'd met in the granite-laden high country of California, around the campfire at the Yosemite Search and Rescue site where I was living in 2009. He was young and full of vigor as he both intently listened to stories and enthusiastically shared his own. His wiry frame seemed to radiate energy as he talked me through sequences of climbs that he had done with seeming ease. They were routes I hoped someday I would be able to climb.

"You just have to commit," he said, describing difficult climbs. "You will never know if you don't try."

Like me, Hayden saw the walls of Yosemite not as a means to an end in itself but rather as a training ground for the high alpine. As the son of the great American alpinist Michael Kennedy, he had grown up on stories of the mountains of Alaska and the Karakoram. To those around him, including me, it seemed predestined that he would take his talents to the high peaks.

We stood drinking beer around the raging campfire at the YOSAR campsite as it emitted light into the dark ponderosa forest. I was sure all my teammates shared my view of Hayden as the golden boy, the climber who, if he wished, could define his generation.

Months later, Hayden and I found ourselves underemployed and hanging around the Front Range of Colorado, with plenty of time to meet up and climb on the granite walls of Rocky Mountain National Park. We walked through the night to the base of a wall we intended to climb. As we moved quickly up the trail, we chatted about mountains near and far, filling hours with stories of climbing and dreams of attempting new routes on rock towers and faces on high mountains peeking out above mysterious foreign lands.

We tied in as the hues of sunrise started to illuminate the face above us. Swinging leads, we moved up the wall. As I led, I felt in control and patient, considering the vertical terrain above and trying to pace my output to reach the next anchor with power to spare. I watched Hayden lead sheer pitches of rock in the thin, high air—it was clear that he didn't need to worry about his power. He flowed over the gray stone without effort, taking each move in turn. At 19, Hayden already had a level of strength and confidence that few climbers ever achieve, and he was only just getting started.

"This is awesome!" he called down, while hanging from a hold just below the crux, a big smile spread across his face.

Consistently, on Hayden's leads, he took the rope to near its full length. When he called "On belay!" from above, it was my job to simply hang on.

As we climbed together, we found a symbiosis in our partnership and talked often of what climbers called the Greater Ranges of the world, a term that originated in the Victorian period, used to distinguish the high peaks of Asia from the European Alps. These were the ranges that held the biggest and baddest peaks to be found on planet Earth—the Karakoram and the Himalaya. Neither of us had been, and the conversations were a combination of giddy supposition and attempts at reasoning why we belonged there.

We were young men driven by action, so we made plans to travel to Nepal in 2010. We would spend the post-monsoon season there, chasing first ascents. Having already seen success on the peaks of Kyrgyzstan, I felt that this was a logical next step. We researched objectives and settled on the plan of starting in one of the valleys adjacent to the famed Khumbu Valley, before joining a third climbing partner to attempt one of the biggest walls in the area.

It was a more expensive trip than either of us had ever taken, so we worked extra jobs and applied for climbing grants, some of which we, amazingly, received. The plan was ambitious, but the audacity of our youth made it all feel feasible.

Before our departure, Hayden's parents, Michael and Julie, invited me to join the family for dinner. Sitting in their home, nestled in the Roaring Fork Valley of Colorado, I was prepared for a grilling about my experience but found them very friendly as they asked me about my background. Where had I started climbing? What did my parents think of it? They were exceptionally fond of their son and understood the path that lay before him, better than Hayden or I did. Michael, in particular, knew about the powerful partnerships that could come from spending time together in the high hills. But he and Julie also knew it could end in disaster.

"Maybe you have read the article in *Climbing* in which I said I would murder the first person who put crampons on my son?" Julie asked.

Tentatively, I said that I had.

She laughed. "Well, I don't feel that way anymore, but I do want to make sure that your top priority is coming home safe."

I assured her it was.

The trip started well, as Hayden and I landed at the Lukla airstrip and charged into the mountains. Above our heads, the clouds swirled around impossibly high peaks. Our approach along the trailheads into the Khumbu Valley—above which rises Mount Everest—was swarming with Gore-Tex- and leather boot–clad tourists whose goal was to hike into the roadless valley, to hear the monks chanting at the local monasteries, and simply lay eyes on the massive peaks.

We were just as impressed by the views but not satisfied to sit and look. We felt a deep need to experience the walls surrounding us with our own hands and feet. As we walked, we discussed strategy for our planned ascents. I felt superior to those tourists around us—we were there to *climb*.

Hayden's talent and strength were infectious, but just as infectious was his ability to balance his ego against genuine kindness and concern for others. Even as we talked about how low angle Everest looked, he was kind and inquisitive to the people we encountered heading toward the thriving base camp at the head of the valley. We heard it described as a small city inhabited by tourists and their hired staff, full of large colorful tents featuring satellite internet and above which fixed ropes led to the summit of the highest peak on the planet. I watched his balancing act and wondered at my own motives as we headed for a much quieter part of the range.

Like many before us, we found that the mountains had very different plans for us. The peaks we chose for the start of our trip were steep and our strategy was poorly refined. Unlike Yosemite, the cracks didn't connect; and unlike Alaska, the ice didn't connect. We had planned to arrive and scope routes from the ground but found ourselves lost as we tried to trace lines up the chaotic mountain walls around us. The size of the features—true to their reputation as "Himalayan in scale"—kept us from approaching them without knowing exactly where we would go, something we didn't know how to determine. Simply put, we were entirely out of our league.

Overwhelmed by our surroundings, we sat at our little base camp by the picturesque Gokyo Lake. Hayden succumbed to a bronchial infection, likely picked up from the burning cow dung that was used in the villages for cooking.

In a fit of bravado, I decided to attempt soloing a route. I set out with a heavy pack, walking alone along the lateral moraine until the path forward forced me onto the glacier. At its edge, I set down my pack and sat on a rock, looking out across a web of crevasses in the ice that were covered by thin snowbridges. I picked out a line through the terrain. *Maybe it will be fine*, I thought, *but if I had a partner, we would certainly wear a rope*. I sat there for a long time, but no amount of waiting would change the hazardous terrain before me.

I walked back from that attempt under a full moon, having hardly made it through the approach. I both chided myself for being gutless and was pleased I had made a safe decision. Eventually, I let it go and just watched the moon and stars pass over me as I walked.

Looking back up the walls above, I was forced to accept that it had not been technical climbing that had defeated us. We had been turned back by the scale of the landscape around us; we were too green to comprehend the strategies needed to ascend such enormous walls.

Still, as we departed the Gokyo, I felt we had made good decisions. We were acclimatized and had another peak in our sights, and I had kept my promise to Hayden's mom.

The second phase of the expedition kicked in when we joined our third partner, Cory. Our base camp was situated in the hills above Dingboche, a small village built into the hillside out of stones and rough-hewn poplar trees that blended with the environment. Above camp, the immense Cobweb Wall on the south face of Nuptse hung over us. It was a dark wall streaked with white dikes, too steep to hold much snow. Hayden found himself overwhelmed, understanding that he was not yet ready for an objective that severe. I let the immensity of the face consume me with excitement and fear as I strained to picture myself weaving my way among the massive snow flutes and rock buttresses. I drank coffee and rattled on with excitement and a distinct lack of both experience and strategy. My young, fired-up energy jived poorly with Cory. In the end, discord between the two of us, along with poor conditions on the face, sent us all home early.

I was devastated. I felt like I hadn't even been provided the opportunity to try. My partnership with Hayden had started out promising, but the trip had been a major hiccup.

Back in Seattle, injured, grounded, and reflecting, I felt I had failed rather than succeeded in surviving my first encounter with the highest mountains of the world. Likewise, my partnerships had fallen by the wayside, and my progress in the big hills—or any hills for that matter—had ground to a halt. Hayden called to check in from his latest climbing trip, and we remained in touch, but as I watched him quickly progress, I was left with a deep-seated fear of being left behind.

▲

THE INJURY I sustained in New Zealand laid bare the lack of sustainability in my lifestyle. I had nothing to offer and no foundation—outside of what I was fortunate enough to be provided by my family—and I had no plan for how to do anything other than continue pursuing climbs.

Through the lore of the climbing community, I had been indoctrinated into a culture that asked for climbing to be everything. Around the campfire in Yosemite, I had heard stories from the scene of the 1970s and '80s, which although decades before my time, told me to give up on the world and engage with the simplicity of ascending soaring rock walls. Meanwhile, books like *Savage Arena* by British hardman Joe Tasker had indoctrinated me in the ethos of modern mountain climbing or, as we call it, alpinism. This culture told me to actively fight the mainstream by dismissing the vanities of materialism and instead search for my limits in some of the world's most hostile terrain. But I was finding that there might be a need for something else, something to offset the pursuit of climbing.

As I stared ahead at almost a year of recovery time, my parents patiently looked after me while letting me stay at an apartment they owned in Seattle. Normally, it was used by my father when he needed to stay in the city for work, but knowing that I had nowhere else to go, they accommodated their wayward son and let me inhabit it for the worst of my recovery. They checked in regularly, making sure I had what I needed, but three PT appointments a week and daily exercises left me with many hours to occupy. Normally I would have filled them with training, but I could barely handle a nightly ritual of walking two blocks to see the view of the city lights.

The apartment was in an old brick building with accents that harkened back to the 1920s. I was physically comfortable, but there was no mental comfort. I tried to dedicate my time to quiet soul-searching but worried I was getting soft and losing my edge. Some days I just ended up stoned.

Friends from my past in the city showed up to help but, despite their best intentions, visits were infrequent. Many of them were busy building careers and families. I had considered my own path more radical and righteous, but as I sat, broken and indebted to my parents, I envied the security of their well-grounded lives and relationships.

Most of my old friends were on a steady trajectory toward success. Meanwhile, I was pursuing some kind of pinnacle experience, a moment when opportunity, fitness, and geography would all come together in my favor. But I spent more of my time in the troughs between those peaks of perfection—working, toiling, planning, and training in preparation. There in that apartment, I found myself in a particularly deep trough, and the gentle nods I received when I tried to explain my goals left me frustrated and embarrassed.

Nick Neiman was the exception. He and I had been introduced through family friends two years earlier; I suspect they saw us both as idealistic eccentrics. Our friendship had started with a late night of yelling.

"Fuck it, they're all posers anyway," I had yelled at him over the din of a party, not properly attributing the quote to Mark Twight.

Nick grabbed me by the shoulder and yelled back, "*That* is what I'm talking about!" We became fast friends.

In 2012, Nick was slogging through post–art school career development. It looked like a hard impact with reality. He swung by the apartment after his workday had ended to cook dinner and hang out. Over food and drinks, we discussed the world and our futures.

"Man, capitalism is so antithetical to creating anything new or worthwhile," he muttered.

Nick's creative background was starkly different from mine. He saw the world as a series of stories and compositions—the flow of a hero's journey alongside the rule of thirds and the golden mean. My perspective was deeply rooted in science: form a hypothesis, make a prediction, test the prediction, iterate forward based on the results.

Over late-night bull sessions fueled by cheap Manhattans, poorly rolled joints, and Thelonious Monk, we discussed these views on the world and how they related to our past and our future. At first, the perspective of the artist felt contradictory to that of the scientist: he saw my view of the world as rigid; I saw his as squishy and lacking rigor.

Eventually we found that our conflicting viewpoints represented an objective versus subjective view of the world. Science was the system of acquiring knowledge, whereas art expressed knowledge—even if that representation was subjective.

One night after Nick left, I sat up late, considering how this perspective could be incorporated into my budding career as a sponsored climbing athlete. I started to see the mountains not only as a problem to be solved but also as a canvas on which I could lay down a brushstroke. I was being asked to present and write on my climbing, and within this I saw potential to make my stories stronger, to make my messaging more potent, while keeping the subjectivity reined in so they were still true.

Considering this, I wondered if this sense of balance could also strengthen other parts of my life. Could I create a path forward in which I could maintain a relationship, be a contributing member of society, and still pursue climbing? Would it make me a better person?

I hated the temporary disability caused by my injuries, but in retrospect, it seems more like a boon. It took eight months of hard work with a physical therapist to get back on my feet. During those months I had time to step back and consider my path forward.

I meditated on how I could find balance between climbing and the relationships I craved. I daydreamed about a stable life. I read about other climbers and tried to look beyond their résumés of ascents to see what kind of people they were. I saw that some of those I had idolized were worth setting aside, while others rose to new significance as I weighed their climbing against their contributions.

I also spent hours poring over maps and images, looking for the objectives that I could use to define my vision of what I was capable of in the mountains. And as I regained my strength, I felt the pull of those mountains. Subsequently, my need for balance became easier to ignore.

After a stint working on another geology contract (I needed money), I headed to California to train.

As I moved my body over the golden Sierra granite, its coarse grains felt familiar under my fingertips. Climbing seemed like a precious gift that had, at long last, been returned to my grasp. Despite not being challenged by the moderate routes prescribed by my physical therapist, I delighted in the sunlight, the expanse of mountains extending beyond the horizon, the exposure falling away beneath my feet. And the silence of the wild spaces was a welcome departure from the constant noise of the city. From the months of brainstorming in Seattle, I had come away with the framework of a plan. I was going to continue with my climbing and explore creativity—and I was going to become a fully professional climber.

▲

IN THE EARLY 2010s in the United States, there was, essentially, one place to obtain sponsorship as an athlete. It was the nexus where all the climbing companies met: the Outdoor Retailer trade show in Salt Lake City. With a pass secured through a friend and my climbing résumé in hand, I headed there to pitch myself as an athlete. No longer would I be held back by distractions. I was determined to go pro.

Having washed in a river and pulled on my best plaid shirt on the way into town, I pushed through the glass doors of the Salt Lake convention center. I was instantly assaulted and amazed by the sound of thousands of conversations happening all at once in a quarter square mile of branding, advertising, product, and swag. Signage indicating the location of different vendors and brands hung from the lofted ceilings, competing for space and attention. Below them were hundreds of booths, each designed to reflect the brand it housed and stuffed with the latest equipment and technology. I recognized many of the companies, but the climbing brands I was looking for were not visible. From the entrance, various corridors led to hordes of people chatting and hustling. With no clear idea of where to go, I strode in confidently, attempting to look like I belonged.

After an hour of wandering around, I found what I was looking for in what people were affectionately calling the "climbing corner." It was here that, having won an award and been featured in climbing magazines, I was sure people would recognize my face and name.

Larger-than-life images of climbers graced the walls of booths containing the latest—and supposedly greatest—climbing gear. Screens showed videos of people rock climbing in T-shirts, crimping small holds in the sunshine. Photos of people in the mountains were harder to find, but after some searching I found images that showed the practice of climbing I was enamored of: high in the mountains, sometimes in the sunshine, other times in the snowy swirl of a storm.

At the front of each booth was a desk with a staff member acting as gatekeeper. I knew I needed to talk to the marketing teams and athlete managers. And in order to meet with these folks, I needed to start with the front desk.

Being picky about equipment and brands, I chose my targets and went to each front desk asking if I could meet with anyone from their team. Consistently, I was told, "So sorry, but it looks like their schedule is totally full." Leaving my résumé, I asked them to pass it on. Smiling, the gatekeeper always said they would be happy to. Even the brands I already had preexisting partnerships with—all of which were small and uncontracted—didn't have time for more than a handshake and a hello. More often than not, I was offered a coffee. By noon and after a dozen rejections, I was highly caffeinated and my stomach was a deep pit of hunger. My plan of getting set up with sponsors was going poorly and I did not want to waste any more time. I took passes by the energy bar and nutrition brands, taking samples to satiate myself. On a diet of bars and more caffeine, I continued my campaign.

Eventually, I was offered an invite to one of the evening parties taking place after the show. I hoped this would be an opportunity to meet with the managers who held the keys to sponsorships. Away from the corporate hubbub of the show, I hoped they would recognize me.

As the day wound down, and the offers of coffee transitioned to offers of beer, I started to sit back and watch. From what I could tell, most of the people coming and going from the booths had prearranged meetings. As I talked with folks in the aisleways between the booths, I gathered that most of them were not there to ask for gear or money; rather, they were looking to spend. I also saw a number of other athletes wandering the halls, stepping in and out of meetings, so I was not totally off the mark thinking this was the place to be. I just needed to get myself in front of the right people.

The first day of the show wound down and everyone dispersed to the myriad restaurants and pubs near the convention center, and then to a series of parties sponsored by the major outdoor brands. It was to one of these parties that I had been invited.

As I walked into a downstairs event space that was meant to feel like a nightclub, I instantly felt out of place, with the electronic music blaring and multicolored lights moving around the walls. But most of the crowd were people who looked like they were ready to go for a light hike rather than dance all night. Some were, in fact, dancing, but most did not know how.

Looking around the room, with all the tech fabric shirts and light joggers, I realized I was in a room of people similar to myself. As I joined in on attempting to drink enough to gain the ability to dance, but only managing the courage to look silly, I was able to connect with people who were glad to talk to a young, up-and-coming climber. Over the thumping music, I yelled stories about the high mountains of the world, but quickly the conversations would fall away from climbing and into the industry of selling outdoor gear. Over the din of dance music, I attempted to listen carefully, seeking any knowledge that would help me navigate the following days of the trade show. But I gained little insight and ended up attempting to dance until late into the night.

The next two days were the same: hours of rejection, caffeination, and intoxication. I never made it past any of the gatekeepers in front of the booths; I never solved the riddle.

On the fourth and final day of the show, I had a meeting with Kaj Bune, owner of the American branch of a Swiss expedition equipment company. He was an old friend of my father's; we had met briefly in Seattle. With a deep well of experience in the big mountains, particularly in Alaska, he had been generous enough to give me encouragement many years before. I hoped he would be able to do the same again.

The halls of brand booths that had a few days earlier seemed so vibrant and full of promise now felt tired and frustrating. Thus far I had come away from the trade show with a sore stomach from eating bars, a hangover from the late nights, and a couple of free pairs of socks. Since it was the final day, there were far fewer people roaming the hallways, and many of those who remained were starting the work of deconstructing the booths. The screens showing climbing athletes cranking in the sun were turned off.

I walked into Kaj's booth and shook his hand. He greeted me with a kind smile and offered another coffee and a sandwich, which I gladly accepted. As we sat down, he didn't ask me how the last few days had gone; instead, to my delight, he asked about Alaska.

Sipping my coffee, I shared with him about my expeditions and my love for climbing. He reciprocated with his own stories from the 49th's ranges. He had explored many of its little-known corners, mostly on skis, making first ski descents of massive yet unexplored mountain features. Unlike my stories that focused on hard pitches, his focused on the sun setting over rugged vistas and strong partnerships. For him, the accolades of success paled in comparison to the camaraderie and experiences.

"Graham, you are on an exciting path with your climbing," he said, "but I want to caution you. I don't know if sponsorship is your best way forward."

He explained that trying to monetize my personal practice had drawbacks.

"It's when you start climbing for someone other than yourself that you lose the love and you start making bad decisions," he kindly advised.

With a patient smile, he asked me to think about why I loved climbing, what about it made me tick, and encouraged me to pursue that instead, not to soil it with money and being a marketing asset.

"Marketing asset?" I asked.

"Graham, when you work for a company as an athlete, you are an asset that they will use to help sell their product. It often has little to do with your goals of personal progression or pushing the practice of alpinism. Instead, it has everything to do with selling your image and success in order to get their brand in front of a larger audience. There's a path in which you can craft these partnerships on your own terms, but it takes time and patience, and it doesn't pay well."

Kaj's manner wasn't that of a parent telling their child they are doing the wrong thing. He was more like a sage providing guidance that could be followed if one liked. Then he got to his main point.

"Your goal, my friend, should be to survive."

Kaj explained that, for years, he had been operating under what he described as the "100-year plan." The idea was that any decision made in the mountains was placed against his overarching goal to live to be a centenarian.

"If you survive to be one hundred years old, imagine how much climbing you can do. Think about how many amazing experiences you can have. Success is survival. The only true failure in the mountains is dying."

"I dig that perspective," I told him—but in that moment I realized I rarely considered becoming old. I was 26 and only occasionally thought about turning 30, let alone ticking over into triple digits.

Do I have a death wish? I wondered. *No, just a case of severe myopia.*

Kaj wasn't telling me I shouldn't try to become an athlete; he was asking me to think about being more than just a climber.

"What do you want to represent?" he asked, while encouraging me to maintain work outside of climbing so I could always step away if I needed. "Don't become part of someone else's brand," he said. "Create your own—and let others buy into you and what you believe."

With the day coming to a close, Kaj gave me a new pack to try out in the mountains and, once again, shook my hand. He asked me to stay in touch and told me he was excited to see where my path led.

I smiled and thanked him, assuring him that I would.

Walking out of the convention center onto the street, I breathed in the fresh air and looked up toward the Wasatch Range that rose just outside of town. I had gone into the trade show hoping to come away with promises of free gear and airplane tickets. Instead, I had come out with a huge reset on my perspective on the mountains, and Kaj's "100-year plan" was motivating—it felt positive and optimistic. But planning for a long life would also require more consideration toward making money, forming relationships, and building stability.

I'll figure that out later. For now, let's see what we're capable of, Graham.

I was physically rebuilt and ready to once again head into the mountains with an eye for creativity and defining my *own* brand, my *own* sense of what I believed and wanted to represent. Despite the risk, despite the injuries—more than anything, I wanted to climb.

4

The
Waddington

Thump. Thump. Thump. The blades of the Bell 206 LongRanger helicopter spun over our heads as it carried us up a deep, forested valley
and over heavily glaciated granite. I sat with my headphones on, staring out the window as the terrain fell away beneath the skids. As the
forest disappeared, we watched the sheer walls of the Stiletto Group
emerge in front of the bulk of British Columbia's highest peak, Mount
Waddington.

The range in front of us was formed by the same massive series of
mountain-building events that had uplifted the peaks of Alaska, the
Cascades, and the Andes. As the Pacific plate smashed into the Ameri-
cas, it forced the continental crust upward into a range broadly known
as the Cordillera. It stretches from the tip of Tierra del Fuego to the
edge of the Alaska Range. Hidden along the remote central coast of
Canada, Waddington is the highest peak in the Coast Range of British
Columbia and was once known as Mystery Mountain.

Staring ahead at the jagged peaks, I thought about the first climbers to explore this range. They had hiked for days through the rainforest to reach the glaciers, subsequently engaging in some of the most epic adventures in the history of North American climbing. Later, with the advent of airplanes and helicopters, climbers had started to explore the severe granite walls that surround the peak. These climbers had found fabulous rock climbing in an immense and remote alpine setting. I was sitting beside my partners—Blake Herrington, Scott Bennett, and Forest Woodward—hoping for a similar adventure.

Scott was a lanky Michigander with a knack for figuring out challenging climbing sequences on the fly. He and I had met in Yosemite Valley early in the spring of 2010. At the time, we were both participating in the time-honored tradition of attempting to live for free in the national park. In the mornings, we would hang out by the bear boxes in a parking lot, a spot dubbed "camp three and a half," since we didn't want to incur the cost or hassle of camping at the official Camp 4 campground. At night we would sneak off into the boulders, trying desperately to avoid the rangers, playing a game of cat and mouse as we dodged their headlights and ducked into the woods. During the days, we experienced what was to us ultimate freedom: attempting the amazing walls that sprang from the valley floor.

Our partnership had started over coffee and quickly escalated to climbing El Capitan's *Salathé Wall*. The pitches of the classic route fell away below us with ease as we transitioned between making upward progress with our hands and feet and stepping into nylon ladders connected to pieces of protection that we placed into the wall's continuous crack systems. Reaching the top of each pitch, the lead climber would fix the rope to the anchor and start to drag a haul bag, affectionately known as "the pig," filled with water, food, and sleeping equipment. The second climber would then connect their ascenders to the line and climb as quickly as they were able, trying to beat the haul bag to the anchor. This would be repeated from breakfast until dinner, when we would stop at one of the route's ledges.

In the evenings, we would sit on our small ledge with feet dangling over the abyss. As we ate a simple dinner of crackers and canned chili, we would watch the sun set over the mouth of the valley and chat about the climbs we dreamed of completing around the world. We found quickly that we had a similar interest in adventure and exploration of the unknown.

After three days, we topped out the wall and returned to the valley floor.

The following morning, we were sitting by our respective bear boxes when the rangers pulled up.

"Listen, guys, we know what you're doing. We've got our eye on you."

We feigned ignorance, stating that we had just arrived in the park. They looked us up and down. With no showers available, we were still dirty from the wall climb. We were kicking back on the tailgates of our trucks in an overflow parking lot—a telltale sign of long-term illegal habitation in the valley. Unofficially, climbers like us were on the rangers' troglodyte list of cave-dwelling creatures.

"It's probably best that you leave the park," the ranger said with a stern look. "We're going to catch you and you'll never be allowed back in."

We quickly made plans to vacate Yosemite.

Driving south, we headed to the Needles, a series of high-altitude granite spires east of Fresno. With free camping and no rangers, it was a place we could relax before I started work on the Yosemite Search and Rescue team and Scott headed back onto the road.

Soon after we'd arrived, rain poured over the ridge of spires. We built a huge fire, and as we sat warming ourselves, patiently baking bread in a Dutch oven, we discussed our favorite authors. I had been reading Tolstoy and Melville, Scott had been reading Hemingway and Rand. We exchanged books from the small libraries we each had in our cars. I gave Scott *War and Peace*, while he handed off a copy of *The Fountainhead*.

▲

BLAKE AND I originally met briefly in New Zealand and then reconnected during a brief stint in which I was attempting to live in Boulder, Colorado. On our initial foray into the mountains, we quested up a new route in Rocky Mountain National Park. On a traverse pitch, I bashed a thin beak piton into a seam in the granite and looked ahead at the unknown moves across a face to another crack system. I glanced back at Blake. "I've got you—go for it," he said confidently in his signature serious manner. Crimping and gastoning through the face, I balanced on small footholds and made it to the crack. I placed another piece of protection and looked back at Blake; he was grinning.

I did not last long in Boulder. The combination of trying to train, climb, work, and date wore me down. Ultimately, my dear friend Joe, on whose couch I was sleeping, kindly asked what my plans were for finding my own place to live. But my friendship with Blake, and also with Joe, continued as I headed out on another geology contract and to climb in other parts of the country.

Now the three of us, Scott, Blake, and I, were in a helicopter, on our way to a series of climbs in British Columbia that I had learned about from Ian Nicholson—soaring granite faces with no existing routes and nothing but potential. Blank surfaces on which we could draw our own lines.

Forest was along as photographer. He and Blake had met while working in a remote part of the Washington Cascades and had formed a strong friendship. With a thick mane of long, dark brown hair and a quiet, contemplative manner, he was the very picture of an artist—he had, in fact, been to photography school. On the way to the helicopter landing pad at Tatla Lake, he spent most of the drive in the back seat with his shirt off and the window down, watching the landscape pass, occasionally lifting his camera from his lap to capture a frame.

The helicopter landed at the empty Sunny Knob base camp; we unloaded our gear, holding on to it as the pilot lifted off. We listened as the helicopter flew off, leaving us to the silence of the mountains around us. The weather was perfect and would continue to be for most of the next three weeks.

Forest settled in at base camp as Scott, Blake, and I headed up into the Stiletto Group to attempt an unclimbed route on the west face of a wedge of granite named the Blade. Tied together and walking up the glacier, we watched the face's features emerge as we grew closer. Untouched corner systems and face cracks linked together, heading toward the summit over 1,800 vertical feet above.

Before the trip there had been very little discussion about the ethics of how we would like to climb. We all knew from past experience that we agreed on the style with which to approach these walls. We had no sleeping equipment and no drill for placing permanent bolts into the rock. We wanted to climb these routes onsight, in a push from camp, and to be as free as possible while leaving no sign of our passage.

After a false start on a crack system that dead-ended, we headed up another corner system and made quick progress up the wall. The rock was magnificent but strange; reaching a corner that we anticipated would hold a climbable seam, we found it totally sealed off and unprotectable.

Scott leaned off the belay, looking up the wall to the right. A crack on the face drifted upward through a dike of black rock.

"Guys, I think this will go," he said tentatively, before stepping off the belay and sliding his fingers into the crack one jam at a time.

Blake and I climbed after him, following the crack's path upward. It led into more climbable terrain; we kept going up. I crimped through an intricate sequence around an arête that led into a roof with a thin crack leading out its edge. I climbed into the roof, placed a small cam, and tried to fit my fingers into the crack; they didn't fit. Placing a sling on the cam, I pulled on it and placed another farther along the roof. Once past its lip, I found climbable holds and made a few more moves to a ledge where I built an anchor before calling, "Off belay!"

Standing on the ledge, we looked out over the range. Bathed with sunshine, the Canadian Coast Mountains were overwhelming to take in and full of possibilities. We drew lines with our fingers as we described to each other where existing routes went and where others might go. We had nearly perfect weather and a team that was totally in sync. Nothing felt impossible.

Looking down at the glacier below us, I was brought back to my university years studying glacial movement patterns. The massive Tiedemann Glacier was showing all the signs of retreating—distressingly like most glaciers on the planet. In particular, the icefall leading up to the col between Mount Waddington and Combatant, formerly an easy climb, was looking the worse for wear, with massive ice cliffs and crevasses showing that it was losing mass and collapsing. I thought about the helicopter we had used to access the range, one of the least carbon-efficient modes of transportation available. *We are part of the problem.*

Pulling myself away from concerns of carbon and climate, I looked up at the cracks leading to the summit. I racked up and headed upward.

The summit was broad with room to untie and walk around; we relished having finished the climb. A light haze blew in, creating a stunning ambiance. We took photos of each other in the magical mist, hooting as we held our arms high in celebration. Then the moisture blew away, once again revealing the range around us. After the apocalyptic snowstorms of Alaska and the winds of Patagonia, it was pleasant to sit on the summit in fine weather knowing that we had plenty of time to make it back to camp.

Building anchors and sliding down our ropes, we headed down the far side of the peak. We then followed glaciers and couloirs back to the protruding rib of rock that housed base camp. We walked into camp just after dark, where Forest had a warm dinner of couscous, veggies, and beans ready.

Morning found us tired and ready to rest. We relaxed in the sun, drinking coffee and organizing our gear. Meanwhile, Forest lurked with his camera, never being intrusive or asking us to pose. Curious to understand his creative process, I asked if I could see a few of his images.

He shared images of the three of us going about our morning tasks. It was a familiar scene, but the way he had composed the light, the subjects, and the environment brought beauty to what I considered a rather mundane morning.

"My goal is to simply capture the experience as it happens," he explained. "I don't want to interfere."

He never uses artificial lights or heavy-handed editing. Real life is what intrigues him, not something simulated or acted. For him, capturing the raw composition of surrounding features and natural light is his artistic intent.

It struck me as analogous to my approach to climbing. As I had developed as an alpinist, my goal had become finding the natural lines of ascent that didn't require excessive equipment or contrived tactics. I wanted to ascend mountain features that drew my eye to them—and to do so simply and efficiently. The more trips I went on, the less tasteful I found the large-scale expeditions to the world's highest peaks with their thousands of feet of fixed rope put into place by underrepresented locals. The experience I wanted from my climbing was more elemental: just my partners and me, bonded by the rope tied to our waists, ascending the mountain.

I shared this with Forest, and we were drawn into a conversation that lasted hours. He was also inspired by the mountains and the lines they provided for his eye to capture and his body to move over. Having grown up deep in the ancient mountains of North Carolina, with annual family trips to a remote part of the North Cascades, he knew the alpine landscape well. His hope was to become a better climber, so that he could move over steeper terrain and capture others doing the same.

Over dinner that night, the four of us decided to attempt one of the classic routes of the range, a stunning line in the sky that all of us could climb together. Known as the *Skywalk Buttress*, it had been hailed by some as the best rock climb in the world, an outrageous claim that needed investigating. The climb was all on a steep rock buttress, but to access it would require us to climb the broken glacier I had been looking down on the day before.

The following day, we departed camp with enough equipment for a few nights away. As we approached the steep icefall, more crevasses and walls of ice revealed themselves, making the climb more complex. We stood before it, discussing the best way to approach its labyrinth of holes and cliffs. Eventually, we decided on a route and headed up.

Side-running crevasses and avoiding overhanging ice turned out to be even more complicated, and took more time, than anticipated. Eventually, we were caught by the transition from day into night. Finding a safe place to sleep, we set up our tents and nervously crawled in.

In the morning, as we once again started climbing, a serac collapsed 400 feet to our left. The roar of snow and ice pouring down the icefall was deafening. I stood watching the massive barrage of airborne debris for a few moments before sprinting with my partners to the top of the icefall. When we were finally safe, I looked over at Blake.

"*That's* why I want to focus on rock climbing," he said. "That snow and ice stuff is dangerous."

Reaching the Waddington-Combatant Col, I relished the expanse—and being able to set up camp far away from the hazards found on the peaks rising from either side. We lay out in the sun and looked up at the north face of Mount Waddington with its weaving couloirs of ice, striking buttresses of sheer golden-gray granite, and hanging cliffs of glacial ice. On the other side of the col was the shorter but just as impressive Mount Combatant, with stacked granite buttresses separated by deep, icy clefts. At the center was *Skywalk*.

In the morning, before sunrise, we walked to its base, racked our gear, tied in to the ropes, and started upward. Rather than questing into the unknown, as we had on the Blade, we knew where to go from those who had gone before us. We knew the climbing was well within our abilities; this helped us relax as we ascended. We had fun, and occasionally Forest would stop to hang on the rope to take photos of the rest of us.

The summit was a small wedge of granite. Standing atop it, we looked out over the expanses of British Columbian mountains as the sun started to set. With two routes climbed in such a short amount of time, our normal exuberance at standing atop a mountain had mellowed into a bath of joy and contentment. For a moment we felt like masters of this ferocious and jagged realm, capable of completing anything to which we set our sights.

Transitioning into the descent, we started the process of rappelling down the snow-filled gash adjacent to the arête. At first the descent was simple. We quickly discovered, to our surprise, that where others had found snow and ice, we were finding slabs of rock. Anchors were challenging to build, and we were forced to be patient as we slowly made our way toward the glacier below. Soon we realized that, in our underestimation of the route and descent, none of us had bothered to change the batteries in our headlamps. One by one they all failed, and we were eventually forced to use the small amount of light emitted by the LCD screen on our cameras, alongside the light of the stars, to make the final rappels to the glacier, where we crawled into our bivy tents and quickly fell asleep.

Morning once again found us on the icy expanse of the col. We packed quickly before heading down the way we had come. In the cool morning air, the ice cliffs of the approach to the col stayed quiet, and moving downhill we were able to cover ground more quickly. I wondered to myself if, in the future, I would advise friends not to come this way—tell them that this route, once a standard route, was no longer a safe way to access the peaks above. As we dashed under the final ice cliff and out onto the flat expanse of Tiedemann Glacier, I decided that I would indeed advise folks against this route.

▲

MY EXPERIENCES ON *Skywalk* brought home to me the realities of climate change: the mountains were indeed changing, and the insights and information from the past were no longer always true. Base camps that had been safe were now threatened. Routes that were once easy were now challenging, dangerous, or impassable. We could no longer rely on the wisdom of old and needed to look at the mountains anew, making our own decisions as to what was safe, passable, or not. A warming climate meant that we needed to change our methods as well, otherwise we could be killed.

Back in camp, we made a big dinner and enjoyed the time to rest. Lounging together, we listened to an audio version of the book *A Confederacy of Dunces*, by John Kennedy Toole, about the misadventures of a deeply flawed protagonist, Ignatius J. Reilly, a medievalist academic trying to find work in 1960s Baton Rouge.

The narrator read aloud:

> *I am at the moment writing a lengthy indictment against our century. When my brain begins to reel from my literary labors, I make an occasional cheese dip.*

We all buckled over laughing as we worked our way through another meal of couscous and beans, this time covered in cheese.

Over the next few days, we walked up a to a smaller peak, known as the Claw, that sits above the Plummer hut, a small and robust structure situated on an outcropping of rock among the peaks. It was an objective that we felt Forest could lead. In the evening light, he headed up the arête leading to the summit, placing gear as he deftly moved his feet and hands over the granite. Reaching the small summit, he built an anchor and belayed us up. We all stood looking out at the lengthening shadows that spilled from beneath the summits as the sun rode low in the late-summer sky. There was barely a cloud on the horizon. It had been another day of clear weather in a range of mountains known for their storms.

With the remainder of our time in the range, Scott, Blake, and I took advantage of the continued clear weather and made another first ascent—this time on the peak next to the Blade, known as Stiletto. Finally, we headed up onto the large south face of Mount Asperity, but after seven pitches of poor climbing on decomposing rock, we were no longer having fun and felt that the risks we were taking were higher than we wanted. Deeply satisfied by the trip, we rappelled back onto the glacier and walked to base camp, quoting *A Confederacy of Dunces* the whole way.

The following day, the helicopter picked us up. We loaded our gear, buckled in, and lifted off, once again looking out over the range. This time it felt familiar. We could see the faces on which we had painted our own lines up sheer granite walls. As we flew, the pilot told us that it was exceptionally rare to see such good weather, that we had been fortunate with our choice of objectives and the conditions. As I looked around at my partners, each glued to their window peering out at granite peaks that seemed to reach the horizon—Forest now with his camera clicking repeatedly—I realized it had been nearly a perfect trip.

We landed at Tatla Lake without incident and relished the sweet smell of pines and the lush greens of plants so absent from the high alpine. We drove into the nearest town of Williams Lake with our shirts off and the windows down. We were ready to reconnect with the world, eat some food that wasn't cooked on a camp stove, and drink a beer. Pulling up to a local bar that served burgers, we piled out, tried to make ourselves presentable, and asked to be seated in the sun on the patio.

In what has become a tradition of modern alpine climbing, we found ourselves sitting around a table with our beers and staring into our phones, reconnecting with loved ones, the news, and work. At that time I had been dating a lovely woman from New Mexico. My trajectory, after the Waddington Range, was toward Seattle, where she and I were going to spend a few weeks together before I headed out on my next geophysics assignment. As I sipped my beer, I thought about how nice it would be to see her again.

Leaning back and listening to my voicemails, I had one from my climbing partner Tom Lanagan, asking about winter plans.

"Hey, man! Would you like to go to Newfoundland to climb ice this winter?"

Of course I would. I saved the message and made a note to call him back.

The next was from the owner of the geophysics agency confirming work in central Nevada. Work meant I didn't need to worry about my bank account: *Excellent.*

Last was a message from the woman I was meeting in Seattle.

"Hi, Graham, you should give me a call, we need to talk. I don't think I am going to be in Seattle."

My heart sank. I stood up, taking my beer to the unoccupied side of the patio. Wanting to talk was a terrible sign. From the tone of her voice, it was obvious she was having second thoughts about our relationship.

Finishing the messages, I drank the rest of my beer and ordered another. Forest and Blake looked up, knowing this indicated bad news. During the trip I had told them how excited I was about this relationship. "Maybe she's the one who's going to stick around," I had said.

Coming out of the mountains to unhappy girlfriends—or simply not hearing from them ever again—was nothing new. Being gone for months at a time without contact was a great opportunity for a woman to reconsider whether she really wanted to invest in someone who was heading out on upward of four expeditions a year and spending long stints in places like Eritrea and Nevada running geophysics projects. And how could I blame them? But I had thought this one might be different.

My beer arrived and I called her number.

"Are you breaking up with me?" I asked.

"Wow, what makes you say that?" she replied, startled.

"Well, the tone of your voice and the fact that you're bailing on us spending time together seem like pretty clear indicators."

She was quiet for a moment. "Okay, yeah. I guess you're right."

The conversation spiraled into an explanation of how she didn't want to be second to climbing—not to mention worrying about the obvious hazards of my occupations. I sat with my head in my hands, staring at that now empty beer. She was kind, but firm. None of her concerns were new to me, but I still had not discovered satisfactory answers.

My empty glass moved out of the way and was replaced by a large whiskey.

"I'll bring you another when you need it," Forest whispered, before walking back to join the others.

That night we slept outside of town. Blake had heard about a clutch of rarely visited granite peaks near the border—in particular, a feature called the Deacon near the Cathedral Peaks—and wanted to check it out. We had time. Scott and Forest were keen, I was indifferent.

Blake had been right. As we hiked over a pass, we saw the Deacon, a stunning feature, 1,000 feet of sheer granite with only a single route, one in need of a direct start. Looking at it, I took a deep breath. I had been stewing in self-loathing the entire hike, asking myself if the mountains were worth it. Was I really risking my life? Was I truly undatable? Maybe it would be a woman who would eventually drag me away from the mountains. Maybe I would just be single forever, doomed to become a lonely old man with nothing more than a career of first ascents in remote mountains that no one had ever heard of. But, seeing the striking granite wall, I perked up. Maybe the mountains were just what I needed.

The next day, I found myself let down and unsatisfied as I peeled rocks and soil out of a rotten crack system on the second pitch. The gear below me was wedged into the same garbage and I had no faith in its ability to hold. "This is bullshit!" I yelled as I carefully made moves over the friable vertical terrain. My frustration wasn't meant for Scott, who was belaying; it was meant for me.

Scott led the next pitch and the rock improved, but my attitude didn't. On my leads I tried to climb fast, wanting to get off the feature and get on with my life. We made quick time and rappelled back to the ground.

In the valley below, we lay back in the grass. Scott, Blake, and Forest talked about what a stunning area we were in. I was quiet, wanting to leave but trying not to ruin the experience for my friends.

Soon we were back to the car and driving south over the border toward Blake's home in Leavenworth, Washington. Someone put *A*

Confederacy of Dunces back on the stereo, and my friends laughed at the trials and foibles of the main character, trying to make his way in a world he despised and didn't understand. I was in a similar place: my need to spend time in the mountains made it impossible to maintain the relationships I wanted in my life.

I dropped the guys off in Leavenworth, hugging them goodbye. I apologized for being such a grump; they assured me that they did not mind. By the time I finished the two-hour drive to Seattle, I had transitioned from the roaring guitars of Black Rebel Motorcycle Club to the soothing chords of Mason Jennings. I was exhausted.

Arriving in town, I called Nick, who had looked after me during my injury. He was moving into a new house and offered to buy me dinner if I helped him. I gladly accepted.

His new place was an old mansion situated in a gentrifying Seattle neighborhood. It had a multitude of bedrooms and an expansive living space. Like me, Nick didn't own much, so moving him in turned out to be an easy job. The house, with its high ceilings and echoing wood floors, remained relatively empty. We stood around talking to some of his new housemates, most of whom I had met before. Nick showed me the upstairs, a huge attic that was unoccupied.

"We're going to keep this open so folks can come crash. If you want, it can be a sort of home for you, a place to stay for a little while when you're not on trips."

Nick knew that stability was something I craved but wasn't sure how to achieve. His offer meant far more than a place to crash—it was a sign of true friendship. I was deeply grateful.

We picked up a six-pack of beer and a bucket of fried chicken from a local restaurant—Nick insisting that I looked too thin and needed to eat—and headed to a field down the street where we sat in the sun and caught up. I told him about the trip, how it had been perfect but had all come crashing down upon arrival back to civilization. He listened as I worried that my life was unsustainable, how I was pursuing exactly what I wanted to do, but it was resulting in the loss of people I wanted in my life. I told him about Kaj's 100-year plan and wondered if climbing was really the answer. Maybe I should quit and find something else to do?

Nick reminded me that I was essentially working as an international geophysicist and semiprofessional athlete, that I was, by most standards, extremely successful, making ends meet, and following my dreams.

"Don't quit," he urged. "Just keep working the problem. You've got plenty of time—just survive and you'll work it out."

We watched as the sun started to set and walked back to his new house. We had heard that a friend's Afrobeat group was playing in an adjacent neighborhood and made plans to attend. The prospect of some live music, and my time with Nick, had me feeling better about my future. Maybe I could keep climbing and work it out. Maybe for this evening I didn't need to worry.

Standing in Nick's kitchen, we got to chatting about when he lived next door to the venue we were headed to. It was a small bar named the Sea Monster Lounge that hosted some of the best funk and jazz in town, where musicians were paid a portion of the bar tab, incentivizing us to go often and stay late.

The other housemates were either out or organizing their new living spaces. We had seen all of them except for the fifth, who was a mystery to both of us. Apparently, she was a new member of the elite Women's Ultimate Frisbee team in town named Riot. Then came a knock at the door.

Wearing thick-framed glasses, athletic shorts, and Dansko clogs, in walked Nick's fifth new housemate. She smiled at the two of us drinking beer in her new kitchen.

"Hey, guys, my name is Shannon."

She had just driven up from Corvallis, Oregon, where she was wrapping up a master's in environmental engineering. Having made Riot, she was going to be splitting her time between the two locations for a couple months before committing to Seattle.

"We're going out to hear some music. Would you like to join?" I asked.

Looking down at her book, a thick paperback with dragons on the cover, she said, "Guys, I was looking forward to reading my book, but sure, why not?"

The following morning, Nick poured me a coffee as he simultaneously glared and smiled. A few minutes earlier, I had come out of Shannon's new bedroom.

"Graham, man, I had really hoped that this could be a place where you could hang out when you are in town. But if I am interpreting things correctly, you have fucked that up."

Sipping the coffee, I smiled and told him that I had everything under control.

Nick laughed and looked out the window. "Graham, my friend—I love ya, but you have *nothing* under control."

Dickey, Bradley, and Johnson and the Moose's Tooth. Names like *Ham and Eggs, Blood from the Stone*, and the *Elevator Shaft* resonate with stories of cutting-edge climbing from some of the world's best climbers, stories that defined their generations, demonstrating what was possible at the time. This was where, in 2010, Mark and I had opened the new route *Vitalogy*, our first splash as alpinists.

Looking left on the map, one comes next to the Tokositna Glacier, hemmed in by the head of the Ruth. At its northernmost reaches sits Mount Huntington, with its triangular summit, craggy walls, and perilously fluted ridgelines. In his 1965 *American Alpine Journal* article, famed alpinist Lionel Terray described it as "a beautiful, spectacular and difficult peak, completely worthy of a costly journey across the Atlantic." A true climber's mountain, it is not nearly the tallest peak in the range, but it stands as a siren with no easy way to the summit, attracting climbers to its steep flanks.

Then, the Kahiltna, undoubtedly the greatest of the Alaskan glaciers, for on its margins sit the great three of the range—named Denali, Begguya, and Sultana by the Indigenous people of the Susitna Valley to the south, later named McKinley, Hunter, and Foraker by white explorers. These peaks stand as the sentinels of the range, towering far above the rest and attracting the most attention. The Kahiltna base camp, located at the foot of the easiest route on Denali, the West Ridge, is at times a virtual city. It hosts what is often the busiest airstrip in all of Alaska, with climbers cycling out of airplanes, burdened with hundreds of pounds of climbing equipment, ready to charge up toward the first slopes of the route in an attempt to reach its summit.

On a small rise above the landing strip is another group of camps, where climbers entrench themselves for weeks at a time as they wait for the northern bastions of Begguya to come into shape for climbing. This feature, known as the Moonflower Buttress, is a 5,000-foot wall of sheer granite laced with veins of snow and ice that has, for decades, represented the best and most accessible hard climbing in the Alaska Range. Some of these climbers will also occasionally turn around to consider the massive bulk of Mount Foraker, ringed in seracs with massive ridgelines of snow and ice winding for miles down toward the glacier.

Beyond Foraker, farther to the left on the map, is a region less known to climbers. Winding northward and wrapping behind Foraker and therefore out of sight and out of mind for most climbers are the mysterious Yentna Glacier and its tributaries.

In 2011, the peaks that lie along these glaciers—the Fin, the Bats Ears, the Mantoks, and Mount Laurens—were overlooked by climbers, despite their potential. After our success on Mount Bradley, Mark and I, now hooked on the idea of making first ascents, had been searching for more unclimbed lines in the range.

Our search was a process that piggybacked on the work of climbers and explorers who had come before us, just as their work had piggybacked on the knowledge of the Indigenous peoples who had inhabited these geographies long before the arrival of Europeans. By the time Mark and I were on the hunt, all the terrain in those ranges had been precisely mapped, and, with some digging, we could find images of most of the summits. It was a new age of discovery, more specific and exact. Our job was not to discover what had never been seen but to find what others had never climbed, being either too remote or too hard. Our ultimate objective would be both.

Mark emailed me an off-axis image taken by a bush pilot named Jeff Pflueger of a precipitous triangular face with steep couloirs slashing between granite pillars above the western forks of an obscure glacier: the Lacuna.

The Lacuna Glacier forms a spur off the Yentna and, unlike the other rivers of ice that flow from the Alaska Range, this one had no Native Alaskan name. In the 1940s, climbers had called it Lacuna, Latin for an unfilled space or a gap. Appropriately, the Lacuna remained largely forgotten and mostly untrodden.

While talking on the phone, Mark and I looked at maps of the glacial system. Its icy-blue contours undulated between rocky, gray ridges and faces, showing passes and low-angle glaciers that linked the massive bulk of the Kahiltna to the Lacuna's dendritic and mysterious

Northwest Fork. We made plans to go during the spring climbing season.

As autumn turned to winter and winter turned to spring, I trained in the snowy Cascade Range surrounding Seattle and on the frozen waterfalls of Montana. I dug through archives and spoke with the sages of the Alaska Range, both pilots and climbers. Paul Roderick, from Talkeetna Air Taxis, was only aware of climbing to the east and west of the Lacuna, while Jack Tackle, a mentor and hero, encouraged us to go with that mad twinkle in his eye. This corner of the Lacuna, it seemed, had remained untouched.

Standing before my map, I traced the edge of North America through the frozen breadth of the range. I visualized those big mountains with their thick, permanent layers of snow and ice. In May 2011, Mark and I moved across the Kahiltna Glacier, skiing with laden sleds. Over four days, our world morphed from the familiar zone of Kahiltna base camp, a safe harbor filled with friends, excess rations, and the drone of airplanes, to a zone imbued with uncertainty and the deep silence of open space. Vast swaths of unfamiliar faces unrolled before us as we skied around the east side of Foraker. We stared at icy slopes split by sheer walls of gray and gold stone, finding the few lines that had been completed as we scanned for new ones.

Entering the Northwest Fork of the Lacuna Glacier, we crossed a threshold, a poorly defined line beyond which our knowledge of the terrain was no longer informed by preexisting data. Direct observation became our only guide. We tuned in to our environment, feeling the snow compress beneath our skis and listening to the deep rumblings of the glaciers and the walls. On day three, we were greeted by the 5,000-foot southern and eastern flanks of the unclimbed Peak 12,213, its sweeping gray buttresses pouring steeply down a pyramid of rock and ice. We knew the mountain from the Pflueger photographs, but as we skied forward, it came into sharp relief, revealing the full force of its personality. My joy was equaled only by my intimidation, a fear I would need to repress over the weeks ahead.

Two weeks later, I lay inside our small, green tent while the day's heat warmed the air trapped between the nylon walls. Mark slept next to me in his orange cocoon, with only his tan, stubbled chin protruding. We'd already made two bids at the southwest face of Peak 12,213.

On our first attempt, we started up an obvious line on its eastern margin along a ridge, climbing thousands of feet of steep, loose rock coated with unconsolidated snow. From an unexpectedly pleasant bivy tucked into a nook in the ridge, we launched onto the upper snowy ridge only to be turned around by dangerous avalanche conditions.

Next, we decided to stay away from the snow altogether and attempted the central buttress, a line of sharp arêtes interrupted by thin cornices that drifted over the lower-angle ridgelines. It had started with delicate face climbing, involving placing the tips of our crampons on thin edges, with our ice picks torqued into thin cracks. Higher, we were forced to bash through cornices as we fought up a rocky rib, kneebarring in wide cracks, hooking through thin terrain, and bashing pitons into rock seams for protection. And then, just as we reached the summit snow slopes, a snowstorm rolled in. Our visibility plummeted, the wind picked up. Having chosen to attempt the route in a single push of climbing without a tent, we were forced to go down.

The following morning, we woke to clear skies and a crossroads: we were near the trip's end, with dwindling rations for our two-day ski back to Kahiltna base camp. I separated our food into piles and calculated calories: a few packets of dried potatoes and a handful of bars, enough either for our return or for one more attempt.

"How do you feel about skiing back to Kahiltna without food?" I asked Mark.

From deep within the sleeping bag, a resolute voice emerged: "Let's go for it."

Slowly we scoped for other lines of weakness, seeking a route that would present less-technical climbing and allow us to move quickly. I unearthed packets of instant coffee, pure gold for two young men from western Washington. As we slugged down lukewarm java, I watched

Mark's posture improve and a grin creep over his face. I felt the power surge back into my body. We moved toward the mountain.

While the Arctic summer sun tracked into its lowest position, still peeking over the northwest horizon, we climbed quickly over steep névé. The rhythm of our metal points displacing ice acted as a meditative drumbeat as the dark blues and shadowed whites of the mountain's surface passed beneath our feet, as the concavity of the couloir morphed into the convexity of the summit ridge. The horizon expanded around us, and with it came the sun, now rising. We stood, with the sun shining and a cold breeze blowing. I howled with joy into the biting air currents. It felt good to stand on top—and I was relieved that all our effort had ended with us summiting something.

Taking a deep breath, I stared out at a sea of peaks. "There's still a lot of terrain out here," I proffered.

"Absolutely," Mark replied, his voice hushed with awe. "I don't think we're finished with the Lacuna."

Looking south from Voyager Peak, our name for Peak 12,213, we saw a steep granite face rising in profile seven miles to the southwest in the Western Fork of the Lacuna. Separated by giant serac tongues, its buttresses struck severely off a flat glacier. My eyes blurred with the cold. The buttresses turned into the tusks of some colossal beast; one serac tongue became its trunk. We'd later name this face the Mastodon, and it would grow in my mind, lurking within the shrouded unknowns on the map, its intricate, towering features awaiting human discovery.

▲

THE FALL OF 2012 found me deep in the basin and range topography of Nevada, running a geology survey. My days were spent with a small team of colleagues taking readings that would be corrected for our altitude and the position of the moon, allowing for the gravitational field of the area to be mapped. Our goal was to find anomalies of high gravity that would serve as indicators of a higher-density material under the ground: gold.

As I carried the equipment from site to site, through the sagebrush and steep, unbleached talus, 600 feet at a time, I was not thinking about gravity or gold. Instead, my mind oscillated between two things: the pillars of the Mastodon crashing down into the Western Fork of the Lacuna, and Shannon, whom I had met in Seattle a couple of months before.

Nick had not been wrong when he said that I had nothing under control. If I had my way, I would have seen Shannon every day for the weeks following out first encounter. Instead, after drinking coffee with her and Nick that morning, we found ourselves going to the grocery store and then going our separate ways. Due to her school and Ultimate Frisbee training schedule, and a short climbing trip of mine, we had only seen each other once before I headed out for two months of geology work.

Based out of the small town of Battle Mountain, a tiny blip of humanity along the endless section of Interstate 80 that traverses through northern Nevada, I had little investment in my surroundings. Every day started before sunrise with a pressed coffee made in the motel room, the hot water having been extracted from the motel room's coffee machine. In the cold desert air, with a second coffee in hand (this time from a coffee stand), I would drive out with the crew to a work site as the sun rose. It was in these moments when the day was most pleasant, with the steaks of color from the rising sun turning the desert alive. By lunchtime it was hot and the world around us was bleached. Nothing stirred besides me and my colleagues as we wandered over the landscape.

With my headphones in, I would listen endlessly to Lewis Lapham's podcast, *The World in Time*. Formerly one of the editors at *Harper's Magazine*, he was then running the periodical *Lapham's Quarterly*. On his show, he interviewed academics about whatever he found interesting. When I ran out of energy to pay attention to podcasts, I would just walk and listen to my footsteps moving over the desert, thinking about what I wanted to climb, how I was going to do it, and what I was going to email to Shannon that evening.

The evening emails with Shannon had started incidentally but turned into a slowly moving conversation of carefully considered replies. As each day came to an end, I looked forward to them immensely.

"The stars were definitely better in the Coast Range (fewer trees at camp), but I have to say I enjoyed the crazy understory plants, 40-degree slopes, mapping inaccuracies, and other adventures involved with forest fieldwork," Shannon wrote, telling me about her years spent doing field research.

And we shared the day's victories. "I passed my defense today! Thesis slain. Just dissertation edits next week and I'm done!" Shannon wrote. "Fantastic! Out here, we're now halfway through this project, back to climbing soon!" I wrote back.

In a world of fast-paced communications, it was an unusual ritual that allowed us to stay away from poorly considered responses or misguided sexual advances. It felt reserved, like an eighteenth-century courtship performed from a distance through letters.

Coming home from the field in the late afternoon, I would shower and, with the rest of the crew, choose where we were going to eat. There were only two options in town: Chinese and Mexican, both equally average. After a bowl of chow mein or a fajita, we would retire to our respective motel rooms. I would do a climbing workout, either lifting bags of rocks I had brought in from the field or hanging on a portable hangboard I usually bring along when I travel. After I trained, I would read the email I had received from Shannon during the day. It was generally a simple question and response, gently prodding each other about what we liked, what we didn't like, and what we wanted for the future and how we planned to make it happen.

In her words, she was "finally" finishing school, which was going to allow her to focus on her Ultimate Frisbee career. Having won a world championship in high school and a national championship in college, she was now in the big leagues playing for one of the country's oldest dynasties, Seattle Riot.

Ultimate Frisbee, a highly athletic field sport that combines elements of soccer and basketball, may have been considered a fringe sport at the time, but it was a fringe with which I was familiar. I had, in fact, been conceived in the Kansas Frisbee scene of the mid-1980s and grew up on the side of the field as my dad continued to play competitively throughout my childhood. I was probably able to throw a 175-gram Ultimate disc before I could throw a kid's ball.

So, when Shannon shared that Ultimate was her priority and that she would use her newly minted master's degree to make rent while ramping up playing on the new team, it was neither unfamiliar nor strange. It sounded a lot like my approach to climbing—just applied to another sport, one for which I happened to have a lot of familiarity and respect. When I asked what position she played, her response was, amazingly, in a language that I mostly understood:

"In terms of lines, I played both O and D but mostly D. On D, I play in the front wall of several zone sets and mostly guard handlers/throwers in man D."

This sounded just as nonsensical as my descriptions of climbs. It was fun to pick apart the vernacular and learn the language of her sport. She did the same with mine.

As we emailed, I slowly felt her influencing me in interesting ways. She asked me about my training for climbing and seemed underwhelmed with my responses. Having trained with the University of Oregon Ducks sports program, she had a lot of experience. She made subtle suggestions for my program and, when I applied them, I started to see results.

When I mentioned I was getting sick of the podcasts and music I was listening to in the field, she wryly suggested that I download the latest Top 40.

"Based on what I know about you, you've not heard any of it. Also, have dance parties in the field. I bet it'll make you happy," she wrote.

The following day, in the field, I made sure none of my colleagues could see me while I had a small dance party to Lady Gaga and Justin

Bieber among the low scrum of sagebrush. Shannon was right; it made me feel good.

By the time I finished my contract in Nevada, I was keen for a wider variety of food and a real cappuccino, and to see Shannon. It felt strange to send an email to our long thread of messages stating, "I'm on my way back to Seattle and I would love to take you out for a coffee."

I was delighted to receive the reply: "I would like that."

We met at a snobby coffeehouse, the type of place that has a thick book on the counter describing their philosophy of making espresso, and, if you try to order drip, they will disapprovingly state, "We don't serve that here." We both ordered cappuccinos and Shannon selected a pastry.

Sitting down at a small bistro table, I looked across at the woman I had been thinking about and emailing with almost daily for the past 10 weeks. She was more stunning than I had remembered—even as she tried, only somewhat successfully, to manage the excessively flaky pastry she had ordered.

Our conversation via email had been high level, jumping from topic to topic, like lily pads of courtship. Now we dove in deeper. The conversation came easily, ranging from her work in nano particulates to mine in geology, to the sports that defined our lives. She asked me pointed questions about climbing, not the typical "Why?" or "What's next?" Instead, she asked about training and methods.

"Do you engage with cyclical training?"

"Do you monitor your heart rate?"

"Do you take an off-season?"

Her questions showed that she didn't see me as an explorer or adventurer—she saw me as a fellow athlete. It was a view I found both flattering and encouraging. It was also clear there was a lot she could teach me.

I was staying with my parents. For a few weeks I hung out with them at their home, with regular escapades down to the city to see Shannon. They didn't ask too many questions but had a glint in their eye when they asked if I would be home that evening or the next day. My sister,

Greer, called from Portland. "I hear you like a girl enough that you're hanging around the city?" she asked, before playfully demanding to hear more. It was clear that they enjoyed having me around; they particularly liked the prospect of my being in Seattle more often in the future.

My time with Shannon also meant I was spending a lot of time with Nick. He was incredulous, for we both knew he had not been wrong when he told me I had nothing under control. Unwittingly, he had led me to a potential tether in my unbound lifestyle. I tried my best to be a good friend and invite him out to shows and events in Seattle, but I could tell that he was both amused and annoyed when Shannon was along, as she almost always was.

In the mornings, Nick and I would still drink coffee at the kitchen table, oftentimes with the other housemates Reid, Nora, and Devin. They also were in the elite Ultimate scene. We talked sports, news, and creativity. Having shot a lot of video on my recent trip to Canada, and having been offered use of the footage that Forest had shot, I was working on a short film about my injury and subsequent trip into the Waddington Range. It was a simple story of being injured and coming back. Nick helped me through the finer points of how to compose images and tell a tale. I was deeply inexperienced with editing, but I enjoyed the process as the piece slowly came together.

With winter on its way, I moved into my annual circuit of holidays with my parents and ice climbing trips. In Bozeman, I told my longtime friends from Yosemite Search and Rescue, Emily and Pat, all about this amazing woman I had met. They smiled approvingly. In Ouray, I asked my mentors Roger and John if they thought I should get an apartment in Seattle. Or maybe I should ask Shannon if I could move in? They poured me a beer and wished me good luck. Everywhere I went, with everyone I visited, I talked about this extraordinary woman I had met. Any free time I had away from trips and work was spent in Seattle with Shannon.

Then, as the snow in the mountains started to melt and spring approached, the conversation of how my wandering lifestyle was to blend with Shannon's came to a head. By this time, Shannon's focus on a sport that was not able to pay the bills was also presenting as a problem. She had found some work, but it was only just covering expenses. I was in the opposite situation, with plenty of work but no place to live. Despite it being very early in our relationship—we had only been dating for a few months—it seemed practical for me to move in and for us to share the rent. With an agreement that this was Shannon's place and not *our* place, giving her the autonomy to kick me out whenever she pleased, I moved my climbing gear into the basement and my clothes into the closet.

"See, it was all part of the plan," I told Nick over a steaming cup of coffee at the kitchen table.

He just shook his head.

With the onset of spring, it was also time to get back to work on my project with Mark in Alaska—the peak with no label on the map other than an elevation marker that contained the face we had named the Mastodon. With Shannon's influence on my training, I was feeling stronger than ever and was very excited to give it a try.

It was only once we'd arrived in Talkeetna, in early May 2013, that Mark and I learned from Paul Roderick, who'd flown the Austrian soloist Thomas Bubendorfer into the range, that the peak was in fact called Mount Laurens. In 1997, Bubendorfer had climbed Laurens via its northwest face from the Yentna Glacier. Although Bubendorfer named the mountain after his son, he'd done little to publicize his ascent. The east face of Mount Laurens, which we had seen and called the Mastodon, dominated the unfamiliar West Fork of the Lacuna and had sat neglected in the peripheral view of pilots as they flew toward Denali.

As I stared at the grainy images and contours riding the edges of the USGS Talkeetna D-3 and D-4 quadrangles, the face contorted in my mind. Sometimes, it was perfect: steep, hazard-free, falling from the summit following what the early twentieth-century Italian alpinist Emilio Comici described as the ideal route: "the path a drop of water would take down the mountain." Other times, it was covered in calving seracs and lacked any aesthetic lines. These speculations are a major obstacle in "exploratory alpinism"—the dark of the unknown. To venture into these shadowlands is to take a high-stakes gamble with time and energy. It can pay off massively, with spectacular climbing in unexplored areas, or it can fail miserably, when the intended objective turns out to be too dangerous or simply unattractive. But never to go was never to find out.

That May, we flew by the Alaska Range in Roderick's airplane. Thick winter snows highlighted the strange geometry of the foothills.

"I'm excited that you guys are going to check this thing out," Paul called out over the airplane headset. "What have you been up to since the last time I saw you?" he asked.

I told him I had met a girl. He laughed and nodded his head, having heard this from many a climber headed into the range over the past 20 years of flying. I smiled back, knowing that I had a secret tool along with me—hours of relationship advice podcasts from Dan Savage, a Seattle-based sex and relationship columnist. On this trip, I was going to attempt one of the hardest-looking faces I had ever seen. I was also going to figure out how to be a good partner so I wouldn't lose this new love in my life.

Deeper within the range, we threaded the granite spires of Little Switzerland, behind which loomed Denali, Begguya, and Sultana. Soon, through the windshield a solitary hulk arose: the Mastodon. We swung by the face. Its sheer buttresses and large seracs jutted into view. We could discern climbable lines, but before we were able to follow them to their conclusion, we were off again, to land 10 miles south on a small, unknown glacier. As the sound of Roderick's prop faded, the isolation overtook us like the vacuum of interstellar space, silent, immutable, laden with potential energy. It was uncomfortable but full of promise. We loaded up our sleds, buttoned down our emergency cache, and skied toward the Lacuna.

Every step up the glacier was one step farther into a secret the mountains kept to themselves. I imagined the Mastodon as both a guardian of this realm and a fleeting reward for those seeking its hidden treasures. After two days, we rounded a corner and the east face of Mount Laurens slowly emerged from the surrounding mountainsides. I picked up my pace. Giant seracs poured from the wall, divided by imposing dark-gray buttresses. My chest tightened as I visualized ascending those bastions, silent and stealthy, attempting not to waken the beast. My gaze followed lines of ice and rock, mentally connecting passages that looked climbable with others devoid of visible features.

For a day, we relaxed at base camp. I listened to Dan Savage's advice on how to be a sexual partner who was GGG—"good, giving, and game." We looked at the line, comparing what we could see through binoculars to the images we had taken from the airplane. Now that we were facing the massive wall, it silenced us to near catatonia: a complex 4,700-foot face, its tusklike features dripping with icicles. We opted for the central buttress, the left tusk of the ancient elephant. It swept directly down from the summit in long steps of vertical stone laced with streaks of white, clear of the seracs and cornices that plague so much of the wall. Predicting a three-day push, we packed food and fuel for a lean four, along with a pared-down bivy kit. We planned to sleep during the day's heat, when the mountain was most active, and to climb at night.

A week later, nine days after unloading the airplane, we once again regrouped at our tent, a tiny green pinprick swallowed by the mountains. We'd made two attempts on the central buttress, and we'd turned back twice under clear skies. Each time, we'd climbed thousands of feet of thin seams and anemic flows trickling down corners until the prolonged exposure to poorly bonded ice and drooping snow mushrooms thwarted us. It was simply too much risk. We sat in the sun, drinking recovery powder and staring up at the Mastodon.

"Mark, have you ever considered not going on a trip so that you can spend more time with your girlfriend?" I asked as I dug for our chocolate and bottle of whiskey.

Mark laughed. "My young friend, you have a lot to learn."

I took this as a yes.

"Maybe more importantly, have you seen the chocolate or the whiskey?"

We determined that we had left all of it with our cache of gear at the airstrip.

"Shit."

Having been booted twice by the face, we needed a diversion and decided to reconnoiter other corners of the Lacuna. Four days later, after a storm pinned us down below a small col, we skied back to base camp through three feet of new snow. The Mastodon stared down, tauntingly. I fixed my gaze on the ground, too timid to stare back.

That night, back in base camp, we calculated our rations and slept fitfully as the barometric pressure skyrocketed. The following morning, we saw a millibar reading higher than either Mark or I had ever observed in the Alaska Range. Good climbing weather was on its way. With little discussion, we watched snow shed from the face, slowly exposing the features, both alluring and deadly, with which we were now so familiar. This time we chose a different line—the right tusk, or northeast buttress. It took a series of slanting ramps split by overhanging walls before cresting two towers of rock. The line funneled into the upper reaches of the north ridge, a feature riddled with twisting seracs and cornices.

"It really is difficult to avoid climbing on those classic, terrifying Alaskan ridgelines," said Mark. "But maybe this one won't be so bad . . ."

The first pitch reared up like a standing granite wave. Making careful moves over the bergschrund in the blue evening light, I placed a shallow knifeblade and pulled on thin holds. Two body lengths up, with no other protection, I glanced down nervously to the gaping 'schrund. I downclimbed, perched on the lip, and considered my training, my ambitions, and my desire for a long, lively climbing career. Mark yelled up muffled encouragement. The Mastodon was testing us. We could see that thick ice lay only a pitch above. Taking deep, calming breaths, I pulled back onto the rock.

Sliding my tools upward, I felt for incuts and then pulled down on my picks, one move at a time. I visualized the fall into the bergschrund— my body ricocheting toward the bottom between its hard, frozen walls—and again considered retreat. Instead of broad suppositions based on the unknowns of a USGS quadrangle, I now contended with a microverse, a small ocean of crystals and edges, inconsequential blips between the 40-foot topographic intervals that striped the map but no less vital to our success. I focused again on my breathing. There was a crack another body length away.

I moved up.

Five feet higher, I torqued my pick sideways into the crack and slid a cam into the light-gray granite; with a simple clip of the rope, my body relaxed and my breath moved more easily. The crack now dictated my path. I kept going, placing gear, twisting my tools, and stemming onto thin folds. Sixty feet up, I reached a one-inch-thick curtain of ice. I swung into it and my axe responded with a resounding thud. I let out a whoop and moved up to a sheltered belay cave.

Fifteen hundred feet of rambling ice flows interspersed with rock steps passed beneath our fingers and feet as the sun swung low and then rose again, making the mountains explode with the reds and pinks of the early hours. After many years of climbing together, Mark and I barely needed to communicate as we moved over the terrain. We were strong and our partnership was in sync; it made the climbing feel delightful, like we were carrying out exactly what we were put on the earth to do. In the heat of the late morning, I climbed over a ridge and dug into a cornice. For that day, at least, we would rest well, our tent perched away from the hazards of the wall.

From above our cornice bivy, sugary snow poured over me as the sun set. I pulled out my headlamp. While Mark continued digging through a cornice, my world closed down to leaping columns of illuminated spindrift. After an hour of the rope remaining motionless in my hands, it began to sag as Mark downclimbed; the terrain above was too dangerous, too loose and unconsolidated. To our right, clean, blue seracs jumbled against each other. We rappelled and I moved out into a maze of vertical ice. My tools squeaked as I navigated a citadel of frozen towers and crawled into a crevasse to belay. An obvious path of low-angle terrain led to snow slopes above.

Moving methodically, Mark broke trail. On the summit ridge, we bivied atop a large cornice, passing the time by naming the doomy, overhanging features along the ridgeline ahead as if they were passing clouds: a hulking Jabba the Hutt, an evil Cylon, a sinister bird of prey. To the north was the sweeping arc of the Central Alaska Range—the massive south faces of its highest peaks, with clean, soft light reflecting off brilliant blue ice and stark golden granite. We slept fitfully, the thin tent walls scant separation from the void. When we awakened, the dark purples and blues of the evening were starting to emerge and the same peaks we had been admiring were now partially obscured by lenticular clouds.

Alaskan mountains often hold such surprises high on their flanks. Our final day was spent in prehistoric battle with our Mastodon, excavating through waves of snow. On a section of the map that had looked benign—where wide contours led to a summit only a finger's width away—we pushed sideways. The mountain's apex was just a few hundred feet above.

Finishing a rope length of climbing, I dug a hole and climbed into it to belay Mark. There was no other option for an anchor. I pulled the rope tight and yelled to him that he was on belay. Searching through my jacket pockets, I stumbled upon my iPod. I had accidentally brought it along. Excited for a reprieve from the intensity of the experience, I put in an earbud and pressed play. Dan Savage's voice came on, calmly advising me to be open to whatever sexual kinks my partner might have. I changed it to Hendrix's "Purple Haze."

As we reached the final rope lengths to the summit plateau, the sun dropped below a thin scrim of cloud on the horizon. An icy wind blew, the sweat of our exertion froze quickly. The cold broke down our ability to make reasoned decisions and, in the dim air, we struggled to find our way onto the summit mushroom. We huddled in our tent on the edge of a crevasse, fighting off hypothermia during the darkest hours. Dawn brought warmth and light, and our route, threading its way up the ridgeline above, became obvious. I led a single pitch of steep rime to the plateau. We trudged toward the top with a lenticular cloud on our heels.

Mark turned around on the summit and brought me in.

"Yes, man!" I yelled into the wind. "This is it!"

Mark just smiled, emanating delight as the sunscreen caked on his stubbled face cracked.

We embraced in the wind. Holding each other tight, savoring that moment—together atop what felt like our own small discovery in that immense topography.

The central range to the east lay obscured, but to the west, mountains unknown to us spread wide, a menagerie of wild beasts. With the haze of a storm building, we hustled toward the descent.

A day later, skiing back toward the landing strip, I cast glances over my shoulder as the Mastodon receded into the surrounding contour lines, becoming just another cluster of densely compacted squiggles. I leaned forward on my ski poles and looked up at an unblemished azure sky above the Mastodon. Closing my eyes, I said a short thank-you to the mountains and received their silence with gratitude. A black speck flew high overhead. A raven, noticing us on the glacier, slowly circled once before continuing west.

We reached our cache at two in the morning. The airplane was due to pick us up at 8:00 a.m. Mark set up the tent as I scrambled around our cache looking for the sorely missed bottle of cheap whiskey and bars of chocolate.

Cozy in the tent, we divided the spoils between us and feasted. We were ready to return to civilization, to tell the tale of our ascent, and I was very excited to get back to Seattle—and to Shannon.

6

Revelations

I sat on the stairs leading out of the kitchen in which I had originally met Shannon. It was where we now lived together, with a group of four other friends. The house bustled around me. The air was filled with the sounds and smells of Devin and Nora cooking. Reid was drinking a smoothie while watching highlights from a recent basketball match. Nick and I were both engaged at our computers, checking email. Shannon was down the hall, folding laundry. My hands still had a residue of climbing chalk from a workout at the bouldering gym a few blocks away.

Every one of us was wearing some form of athletic apparel, having been training or preparing to do so. Most of my housemates were competing at the highest level of their chosen sport. Shannon and Nora were playing for Seattle Riot; Devin and Reid played for Sockeye, the top men's Ultimate Frisbee team. Between them they had dozens of medals representing national and world championships. Their year was defined by the ebb and flow of the season, all leading to the annual national tournament, as well as a world cup that took place every other year.

As Shannon and I built our relationship, I slowly picked up more training methods from her, ranging from seemingly obvious concepts, such as defining an off-season in which my body could properly repair, to the specifics of how to do an Olympic deadlift with proper form. Inspired by our other housemates, I was starting to explore the power of eating my way to success.

I was experimenting with exclusion diets to find what worked best for my body and what was best to avoid. For weeks at a time, I would cut out gluten, dairy, or meat, all the while tracking my macronutrient intake to ensure I was still getting the proper amount of calories, proteins, and fats. I would then add those food groups back into my diet and observe how my body responded. If I had any inflammation or increased recovery time, I would cut it from my diet as much as possible.

After a few months of experimenting, I had my diet refined down to a simple set of inputs that could be summed up as pretty much vegan and gluten-free. I didn't care about the labels; all I knew was that I had lost weight and felt stronger than I had ever been.

It was a stark contrast to my earlier years living at the SAR site in Yosemite and in Alaskan base camps. Instead of late-night drinking escapades, I experimented with microdosing and drank espresso. I was exploring what was physically possible with my body and what my mind was capable of.

Living in a house of athletes was making me a stronger and better climber. I could see it—from the crux mixed pitch on the route with Mark on Mount Laurens, when I had been able to calmly hang on to my axes as I hooked on small granite edges, to rock climbs at my local crag. Routes on which the small crimps and finger locks had felt impossible to hold were instead providing a pathway to the top. Moving into the house had been a stroke of good fortune, on many levels.

As I sat there in the kitchen reading my emails, I was mostly on the lookout for work. With the price of commodities down, my jobs in geophysics had become few and far between. This left me with more time to train, but less extra cash. Having not worked for over two months, I was eager to get back out into the field.

As I dug through my inbox, filled with requests for beta on routes, ideas for future trips, and heavy doses of spam, a subject line from C. Trommsdorff jumped out: "Piolets d'Or/2014 nominations announcement"

I opened it.

Hello, bonjour, ciao from Chamonix/Courmayeur,

In the name of this year's jury, chaired by George Lowe, we are very pleased to announce that your achievements of last year have been nominated for the 22nd Piolets d'Or.

The event will take place in Chamonix & Courmayeur from March 26th to 29th.

We would be very honored if you could be here with us to celebrate our common values!

Christian Trommsdorff

I sat for a moment, rereading the email.

"Hey, Shannon, can you look at something for me?"

She walked in, a partially folded T-shirt in hand. She handed me the shirt, I handed her my computer.

Her eyes scanned the email. Her eyes lit up.

"It looks like you have been nominated for something called the Piolets d'Or. Do you know what that is?"

"Wow," I replied. "I do!"

The Piolets d'Or, the highest international climbing honor, is an award that has been given out annually since 1992. It is awarded to a few climbing teams each year by a jury consisting of some of the world's best veteran alpinists. It is essentially the gold medal of alpine climbing; to be a finalist had been a longtime dream of mine.

We looked up the charter for the award. It focuses on alpine-style climbing: ascents in the big mountains of the world without fixed ropes or stocked camps—just you, your partners, your packs, and the rope tied between you. The award committee considers the style of ascent and the spirit of exploration, and looks for a high level of commitment, self-sufficiency, and technical challenge, alongside respect for people and respect for the environment. It was very well aligned with my own values and goals as an alpinist.

To me, the route on Mount Laurens had been significant. The combination of hard technical rope lengths and exploration was a culmination of what mattered to me in climbing. But to receive notification that one of the highest authorities in the field of climbing felt that it was one of the best routes opened that year was an accolade I had not expected.

I explained this to Shannon and our housemates, and the room took on a new energy of excitement.

"Looks like we get to celebrate tonight!" Devin said.

Looking at the athletes surrounding me, I realized that this group of hypermotivated young individuals had helped me become a better alpinist. Shannon, my world champion girlfriend, had given me the tools to take my physical and mental abilities to the next level. It hadn't been more time in the mountains that had set me up for success; rather, it was a stable relationship and being surrounded by positive influences.

A few weeks later, Mark and I were sitting at the front of a large, old lecture theater in Chamonix, France, before an audience of the preeminent personalities in alpine climbing. We were interviewed by news channels and periodicals including the *New York Times*. The reporter asked, "What does it mean for you to be nominated for this award?"

After a long pause, I answered.

"For me, awards in climbing are not important, but to know that our climb on Mount Laurens is considered one of the best in the world this year is a clear indicator that I am becoming a better climber, and that feels good."

I felt satisfied with that answer. As I had become friends with the other climbers who had been short-listed for the award, including Ian Welsted, Raph Slawinski, Hansjörg Auer, and Ueli Steck, I knew I was outmatched as a climber. Hansjörg and Ueli had been groomed by the European climbing scene into some of the best athletes the sport had ever seen. Their routes represented excellent climbers being in the right place at the right time—in particular, Ueli's blisteringly fast new route on the south face of Annapurna in Nepal. He had completed it alone.

Unlike the Europeans, Ian and Raph were more like Mark and me in that we were not full-time athletes who were wholly supported by sponsorships. Raph was a professor of physics, and Ian was a tree planter, but that didn't hold them back from being at the top of the Canadian climbing scene; their route on K6 West in Pakistan was a testament to their strength and experience. Mark's and my explorations of a remote clutch of Alaskan mountains felt paltry by comparison.

I was exceptionally proud of the route we had climbed. I was honored to be included in the celebration. When comparing the objectives in my mind, however, I felt out of place. But there was a glimmer that I was closing in on the bleeding edge. I let myself project forward to a time in the future when my experience and training could make me comfortable in the ranks of the best in the world.

I could also see, for the first time, an attitude toward climbing that moved away from the hypermasculine, holier-than-thou perspectives held by some in the generation before mine. These men I was spending time with were just as dedicated to defining the edge of what was possible, but they were humble. Before the ceremony, as a parade associated with the awards ran through the small Italian town of Courmayeur, Ian and I ducked away to find some peace, quiet, and espresso. There was no chest-beating as we chatted outside the small bistro, just a deep enthusiasm for the wild experiences that could come from the mountains. It felt good and it felt true, a new perspective based in love and freedom rather than darkness and fear. *We are all headed in this direction together,* I thought; *this is where we want to go.*

Assuming that when the awards were announced we would not be included, I didn't bother to wear a nice shirt to the ceremony. And I was right. Ueli, Ian, and Raph were handed the award; Mark and I stayed in our seats. It didn't matter. Once again, just like when Mark handed me that copy of *Extreme Alpinism* 10 years before, I had been exposed to a new level of what was possible in climbing. I knew I could do better—and I thought it likely I would be back.

Climbing was evolving. Two years prior, while climbing Cerro Torre—a towering peak of granite in the Patagonian Andes—Hayden Kennedy, with Canadian climber Jason Kruk, had removed an unsightly line of about 125 metal bolts that had been put in place in 1959 by Italian climber Cesare Maestri. The removal of the bolts was polarizing. Some saw the action as disrespectful; others saw it as good riddance. I thought it was heroic.

I was surrounded by examples of how I wanted to climb and the impressions I wanted to leave. All I needed to do was continue to improve, and to survive.

▲

A MONTH LATER I was once again in Alaska, excitedly looking out the window of a Super Cub. I was flying in with Clint Helander, heading into a little-explored part of the Alaska Range known as the Revelations. I watched the horizon, studded with jagged peaks, as we raced over the tundra.

Clint and I were a similar age but his intensity of character, alongside his shaved head and perceptive eyes, made him seem older. He was more of a frontiersman. Originally from Seattle, Clint had moved to Anchorage at the age of 18 in search of adventure. He found it in the Alaska Range.

Similar to my forays into the Lacuna with Mark, Clint had been searching the periphery of the range for unclimbed gems in unknown areas. This search had led him to the Revelations, a small clutch of steep mountains at the far southwestern edge of the range, just north of the Swift River where the arch of peaks surrounding the Susitna Valley turns into the Aleutian Mountains, which shoot out the Alaskan Peninsula and into the North Pacific, subsequently becoming the archipelago of the same name.

The Revelations were initially explored in 1967 by David Roberts and fellow members of the Harvard Mountaineering Club. During the 52-day expedition, they climbed a number of peaks and experienced what Roberts would describe in a 2011 *Climbing* magazine article as "the most fiendish weather I would encounter on 13 Alaskan expeditions." They also mapped and named many of the peaks, leaving breadcrumbs for future alpinists to follow.

In the 2000s, when Clint discovered those breadcrumbs leading to the range of rugged peaks and walls, his research showed that it had only been visited a handful of times since the 1967 expedition. They had lain patiently waiting in the intervening decades for a fired-up young climber to discover them. Captivated by grainy images from the *American Alpine Journal,* Clint was just that young man.

What he found was a range of staggeringly steep granite peaks situated above a series of small glaciers that flow out toward the great expanse of the Alaskan tundra on the remote western side of the range. Following in the theme of the range's biblical name, the peaks' names also figured in the final apocalyptic chapter of the Old Testament—the expansive bulk of the Angel, the staggering walls of Golgotha, and the massive, studded ridge of the Four Horsemen.

Over the years, Clint had slowly ticked off a number of impressive first ascents in the area. This was how I learned about both the Revelations and Clint. In his reports published in the *American Alpine Journal,* he included high-resolution images of the walls in the range. I was impressed and reached out.

With Clint's encouragement, Scott Bennett and I took a trip into the range during the summer of 2013, hoping for high-quality rock climbing. And while we managed a first ascent on the east buttress of the peak named the Angel, we also endured two weeks of raging storms.

When we finally escaped, I called Clint.

"We just got hammered by storms for two weeks, but those peaks are amazing."

"Yeah, that'll happen," he replied. "We should go back in the spring?"

"I'm all in."

Our pilot made a slow approach onto an unnamed side glacier off the primary Revelation Glacier and set the plane's skis down on the snow-covered ice. We stepped out and before us rose the massive, unclimbed west face of the Titanic, a 3,600-foot-high rocky shield threaded with lines of mixed ice and rock. It was an objective that Clint had learned about from Fred Beckey, one of America's most prolific climbers. By then, Fred was over 90 years old and had decided that the wall was out of his reach, subsequently deeming it worth sharing. It was a stunning prize for two young men enchanted by unclaimed mountain faces.

We set out on skis in the middle of the night with small packs. We wanted to attempt the unclimbed wall in a bold style, with no sleeping equipment. We planned to complete the route in less than 24 hours.

Above our heads a shimmering display from the northern lights wove green and purple strokes of color across the night sky. It transformed, twisting and shifting at a barely perceptible pace. It felt dreamlike as we skied across the glacier and watched the aurora move in parallax against the peaks on the skyline.

The day before, we had made a reconnaissance of the face and had seen a pear-shaped couloir of snow that narrowed into the granite bastions above. Under those northern lights, we followed our ski track to the base of the route, where the wall above eclipsed the sky. We clipped on our crampons and started climbing.

The direct sunlight of dawn caught us as we pulled out the rope and tied in for the first pitches on a mix of rock and ice. It gradually steepened to vertical, forcing us to torque our tools in cracks and wedge our bodies in snow-filled chimneys to make upward progress.

Despite having never climbed together before, we moved well. Our styles of climbing were cut from the same cloth. We were in sync and talked little as we swung between leads.

The steep terrain quickly fell away beneath our feet. With so little equipment, we were not burdened by heavy backpacks. Using this to our advantage, we didn't bother to stop, opting instead for continued movement.

Higher on the wall, the ice disappeared. We alternated between hooking with our ice tools and jamming our hands into cracks. The frontpoints of our crampons screeched against edges on the granite. The quality of the rock was excellent.

The last hard pitch of climbing ended on a nearly flat ridge. The day was then moving on toward evening. Having stopped to brew water on our small stove, we sat, rehydrating and looking out over the range. To the south we could see the intimidating unclimbed north face of Jezebel streaked with ice and heavily laden with hanging seracs; beyond it soared unclimbed Peak 9,304 with a sweeping couloir running up its northwestern arête.

"Clint, this place is amazing."

"Right?" Clint answered. "And to think that these peaks represent just a sliver of the potential for new routes in the Alaska Range."

The look in his eye made it clear that chasing down these types of peaks was something that he intended to do for the rest of his life. I had the same intention.

It was a quick walk along firm snow to the summit, where we took another quick look at the range. The shadows were lengthening, and the colors were fading into the dark blues and grays of the later afternoon. Quickly, we started walking and then rappelling down the east face of the peak.

We landed on the glacier below just as the final rays of sun washed over the range. It was nearly nine in the evening. We had been on the move for over 16 hours. All we had to do now was walk on a glacier to the west side of the peak and back to base camp.

In the dark, we walked briskly over the undulating ice of the glacier. I was in the lead. Carefully, I watched as my headlamp beam ran over the flow of the ice; I felt in touch with it. We made our way down, jumping over smaller crevasses and side-running larger ones. I was exhausted, but still tuned in. As we accelerated down the glacier, I felt it wrap around to the west, pointing us back toward our base camp. I could sense where the crevasses were based on the flow of the ice under my feet. I was surfing its frozen veneer, headed for the safety of camp.

We reached our tents after nearly 23 hours on the go. The swirling rivers of violet aurora above us had faded, leaving a clear night. We drank whiskey under the stars as we looked up and quietly considered infinity. When we finally climbed into our bags, sleep came easily.

Two days later we slid upward, wearing mountaineering boots with our skis in touring mode. We were headed for the pass above camp. Feeling comfortable on the glacier, we skied without a rope and reached the pass with little incident. Having unclipped our boots, we stood looking out to the south over a skyline of peaks unfamiliar to my eyes. They were steep, with expanses of bare granite indicating where the angle was too severe to hold snow. Among the gray granite wound webs of snow and ice, offering potential passage through the walls.

In front, directly across the glacier, stood Peak 9,304. Its summit was an alluring wedge of gray and white. Its northwestern arête crashed down toward the glacier. My eye traced a line up from the bergshrund to the summit. It was a proud line. My body was energized by the sight of the peak and the clear weather. My legs felt strong, I was ready to climb.

"Clint, I think we should go for it. Looks perfect."

He demurred, saying he was still fatigued from our 23-hour effort a couple of days earlier. "It does look good, but I think I need to rest a little while longer."

I kept my mouth closed as I felt my ego flare with frustration. I knew that if Clint needed to wait, I needed to wait too. Rather than admit this to him, I clipped into my skis and turned them toward camp.

Skiing in mountain boots was challenging. I made tentative turns down the glacier, stopping regularly to control my speed. I was frustrated over the perceived difference in fitness between my partner and me—and simultaneously chided myself for being a bad partner. Waiting a couple of days to recover would be no problem, and it would certainly help me as well.

I dropped into a steeper pitch of skiing. I was well out of sight of Clint, who had remained at the pass.

"What the hell, Graham?" I asked out loud. "Why are you being such a dick?" I knew it was safer for us to stay closer together, but I didn't care.

It's an odd thing to consider how you are going to react when you are about die, but in that moment, I received my answer. It came in a long string of expletives as the hidden snowbridge beneath me collapsed and I fell into a crevasse. The world slowed as I felt myself bouncing between the walls as I accelerated downward. One ski popped off as my knee twisted. I came to a quick stop, plugged into a constriction in the hole, the wind forced from my lungs.

"*Fuck!*" I yelled again, as I tried to regain my breath.

Taking fast, frantic breaths, I attempted to assess my situation but was unable to move. Light was shining down through the hole I had created, now 40 feet above me. It cast over the crevasse a strange iridescent blue of poorly lit ancient ice. I was alone. Clint didn't know where I was—and, based on my initial assessment, I was both stuck *and* hurt.

I had fallen with enough force that I was wedged in the crevasse like a cork. I was pinned at my thighs and shoulders. My feet, one of which was still attached to a ski, could wiggle against the ice, but just barely. I could feel a protrusion in the ice painfully pushing into my left quad. This was not good.

Fear welled up and I closed my eyes. It would not, however, assist me at all in this moment, so I pushed it away, telling myself that I would be able get myself out or Clint would find me.

Squirming, I tried to unstick myself. But as I moved, I seemed to slip deeper into the crevasse. The fear came back. My heart rate went up, my breathing became tight. Again I closed my eyes, trying to calm myself.

This is bad, this is really bad.

I knew horror stories of climbers falling into crevasses and being irretrievable. Stuck in the ice for a slow and agonizing death. Some had been alone. Others had their partner on the surface, trying desperately to unwedge them from what would ultimately become their icy tomb.

How hard had they fought to get out? How hard would I fight?

I squirmed. I slipped a little farther down. The sides of the crevasse tightened their grip. I closed my eyes and calmed my breathing. *Fuck Fuck Fuck Fuck Fuck.* I tried to meditate, hoping for a miracle as I felt myself starting to get cold.

"Graham!" I heard from above. "Graham! Are you in there?"

From the quality of his voice, it sounded like Clint was looking down into the hole. I tried to look up and see but couldn't.

"Yes! Clint! I'm here! I'm okay, but I can't get out!" I yelled back.

"Holy shit, dude. I'm so happy you're alive," he replied, an edge of desperation in his voice. "Give me a second, I'm going to build an anchor."

I breathed a deep sigh of relief and thanked whatever higher powers may have been available in that moment.

It took Clint over an hour to pry my body from the ice, using a traditional pulley system.

The feeling of being wrenched free from the constriction in the crevasse and then hanging above it was like being pulled from the jaws of death. I kicked off my remaining ski and watched it disappear into the darkness below. I would never see it again and I did not care. I pushed my back against one side of the crevasse and my knees against the other, trying to help Clint lift me. I slipped on the ancient ice, again fully weighting the rope.

When I reached the lip of the crevasse, I scrambled into the warm sunshine and dry heaved onto the snow. I crawled over to where Clint was sitting, tied in to his anchor system and still breathing heavily from the exertion. I dove into his arms, and he pulled me into a deep embrace.

"Thank you," I whispered.

"My friend," he said, "I'm so happy you're alive. Let's get out of here."

PREVIOUS: *Voyager Peak, Alaska* TOP: *Mark Allen high on the south face of Voyager Peak in 2011* BOTTOM: *Graham looks out over Alaska's St. Elias Mountains while descending from Celeno Peak.* (Photo by Chris Wright)

TOP LEFT: *Ian Nicholson and Graham attempting a new route on Riesenstein Peak in the Kichatnas* (Photo by Ryan O'Connell) TOP RIGHT: *Graham and Shannon with Pebble, 2019* BOTTOM LEFT: *Haji Ghulam Rasool, an old friend of Steve Swenson's and cook for our adventures on Link Sar* BOTTOM RIGHT: *Steve Swenson, an inspiration and mentor, with whom I climbed Link Sar in 2019*

A small portion of Link Sar's southeast face

TOP: *Mark Richey on Link Sar* BOTTOM LEFT: *Rasool's son-in-law Nadeem in base camp on the Link Sar expedition* BOTTOM RIGHT: *Rasool's son Fida Ali, another member of our support team on Link Sar*

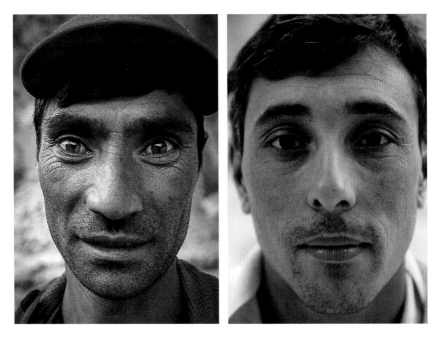

TOP LEFT: *Climbing team member Chris Wright, immediately after the Link Sar ascent in 2019*
TOP RIGHT: *Dave Allfrey high on Kichatna Spire in 2022* **BOTTOM:** *Rainy-day yoga in the Karakoram*

TOP: *A melting glacier near K2 base camp in 2021—one of the inescapable signs of climate change* **BOTTOM:** *Protect Our Winters (POW) in Washington, DC, lobbying for systemic solutions to the climate crisis* (Photo by Elyse Cosgrove)

7

Consequence

[JUNE 2014]

We were nearly two years into our relationship when Shannon brought up the subject of free solo climbing. We were sitting snuggled up on a couch at our home in Seattle, my recently rebuilt knee propped up on the arm of the chair to help with the swelling. We were both reading.

"Hey, Graham, do you ever climb without a rope?"

I paused, looking up from my book, and leaned back on the couch. I was effectively unable to move any more than that, due to the surgical wrapping and the brace extending from just below my right hip down to my ankle—all the result of the crevasse fall in Alaska.

Shannon knew the answer to her question. She had heard me talk with partners about sprinting up peaks and walls untethered, "ropeless and hopeless."

"Well," I said, "not heaps, although I have done a fair amount over the years."

Free soloing has consistently held a special place in the history of climbing, representing complete mastery over the route on which it is being practiced. Over the years, I had occasionally been inspired to leave the rope behind on certain climbs, opting instead for the freedom of moving upward unencumbered. There was no gear to place, no ropes to manage. It was as simplified as climbing could be, just me and the mountain beneath my feet and under my fingertips. Sometimes I had done it with partners, but often I had been alone.

It had started on ice routes in the Canadian Rockies. It was there that I developed a high level of security and confidence while hanging from my ice tools stuck into the frozen waterfalls that cascade from the range's limestone cliffs. In 2009, when Tom Lanagan and I had pulled up to the classic 2,300-foot route *Polar Circus*, it had been late in the day. We had been climbing in the range for over a month. We knew that if we didn't use ropes, we could move up the route faster, so we left them in our bags.

I had climbed shorter routes without a rope, but this one was among the longest and was by far the most serious. I didn't feel any discomfort swinging my tools into the brittle ice. I patiently swung until my picks were well placed. Then I locked off my arm, kicked in my crampons, cleared the lower tool, and repeated the process. Tom and I climbed at a similar pace. We were silent when the ice was steep. We would banter back and forth when the angle lessened and we felt able to put most of our weight on our feet.

On the final steep pitch of the route, the last in a series of frozen pillars, we found ourselves below a party that was climbing the easiest line along the right side of the column. They were sending down barrages of ice, making climbing underneath them too dangerous for our taste. Looking to the left, we could see a far steeper line straight up the middle of the ice pillar. We pulled out the rope, tied in, and climbed dead-vertical ice for the final two pitches to the top.

We made it back at the car well before night fell, delighted with our effort and the level of control we had maintained throughout the afternoon.

"I don't really understand why you would do that," Shannon said now. "It seems so disrespectful to the people who would be devastated if you died. Why wouldn't you just use a rope? It's not that hard."

I thought back to my summers in Yosemite, where my partners and I would ride our bicycles from feature to feature, climbing unroped on hundreds of feet of granite in the evening light. We would sit down on ledges and relish the beauty of our home before turning back to the granite and climbing farther upward into to the golden hues of the setting sun. We felt like masters of the domain, free to climb untethered where we wanted and when we wanted.

Later, I was alone on *Royal Arches* with just a chalk bag around my waist. I climbed efficiently but not hurriedly on the fabled route. It had first been ascended in 1936 and was later named one of the 50 best climbs in the country. For many, it represents their first long route in Yosemite Valley. I had never taken the time to climb it and it seemed like a great opportunity to spend a few hours by myself.

Carefully sliding my fingers into cracks and tapping on holds before committing my weight to them, I made deliberate moves up the 1,600-foot route. I was never out of control and never scared. I didn't listen to anything other than the light breeze blowing past me. I was trying to flow like water over the rock, one move at a time. I was succeeding.

There was no one else on the face. I spent the two hours on route alone in my thoughts. I was focused, I was calm, and I was having fun. A final traverse across a blank friction slab placed me at the top of the route. There I sat on a small ledge looking out over the valley, feeling satisfied, and wondered if soloing was something I would pursue further.

"Shannon, I don't have a good answer to that. It's just something that I've done because it feels good."

"How would you feel about me asking you to stop?" she asked.

I looked out the window of the communal house in which we were still living. It was raining outside, a typical northwestern drizzle. I considered what she was asking. It was far more than just to stop climbing without a rope. She was asking for agency in my decision-making, specifically around risk in the mountains. It was a subject on which I was always happy to take advice. It was advice I often implemented, in the same way I had adopted Kaj's concept of the 100-year plan. But I had not allowed anyone the agency to tell me to do or not do something in the mountains, and no one had asked for it.

I looked at Shannon. She looked back at me.

I then looked down at my legs. The left leg was horribly bruised from the perforated IT band, and the right knee was a mangled mess from ACL surgery. It was an injury that could have been avoided if I'd had a rope on. It was also an accident that could have been much worse.

"Shannon," I replied, "if you'd like me to stop free soloing, I'll be happy to. I appreciate you asking."

It was later that same day when I realized I truly meant what I had said. The idea of no longer climbing without a rope because my girlfriend wanted me to had initially felt lame, like giving in to what the world wanted from me. But as I sat there, broken, I realized that a woman who cared deeply for me was asking me to put the most dangerous form of climbing behind me so I might stick around a little longer. She wanted to invest more in me, and in us, but to do that she wanted to help me survive.

Research in brain science has uncovered that the prefrontal cortex is the part of the brain where humans take on complex behaviors, including planning and truly understanding the concept of consequence. This research has also found that this part of the brain, located at the front of the frontal lobe, behind the eyebrows, is one of the final parts of the brain to finish developing. It is a development that comes to completion significantly earlier in women than in men.

When Shannon asked me to stop free soloing, she was 26 and I was 27. At that time, her prefrontal cortex had long since completed its development, whereas mine had just recently reached the finish line. The increased stability of our lifestyle and the mandatory downtime imposed by my injured knee had forced upon me a potent time of self-reflection and planning. With this new part of my brain online, things looked a lot different than I remembered from the previous time I had been injured, while ice climbing in New Zealand. That had been an experience rife with ignored learning opportunities.

Sitting with my damaged knee, I had been reviewing my recent past through a similar lens. It had been a revealing exercise. I was not delighted with what I saw.

Four years before, when I had started working on a geophysics crew, I had been sent on a job to the wilds of the small African nation of Eritrea. Every morning I woke up to the cool haze in the hours before the sun rose over the rugged eastern Sahara. We were on the edge of the East African Rift System, one of the geologic wonders of the world, where the smaller Somalian plate is pulling away from the much larger Nubian plate that makes up most of the African continent. I would stand on the hillside adjacent to the cinder block shack in which I was housed and sip instant coffee, watching color slowly wash into the horizon line.

I was working with two Mongolian teammates, professional geophysicists Zalu and Togi. They were immensely strong and intelligent men. Togi spoke no English, Zalu only a little. We would drive in a line of trucks out onto the desert floor. The rising sun shone through the dust trails behind the vehicles, creating sharp rays of light that blasted through the cool, dry desert air. It was as magnificent as it was bleak.

The morning was spent walking from site to site, each of us with a separate crew of Eritreans, including a few soldiers. We were taking readings of the specific gravity at locations along a grid of coordinates. Each of the men was wiry and thin, the physique typical of people living in a place of extreme scarcity and poverty, forced to survive on their own in this barren landscape. They all walked at a determined but moderated pace. The crews carried all the equipment; the soldiers carried only their battered Kalashnikov rifles. The government of Eritrea ruled over the lives of its citizens with an iron fist. Many of the crew members had scars from wars fought on the government's behalf. They were stoic, with an intimate knowledge of the land and how to navigate the steep crags covered in woody thornbushes.

When we encountered other locals along our path, they would speak to each other in Tigrinya, a language similar to Arabic but unique to that corner of the world. They would point to me, a curiosity with my white skin and clothing made from technical fabrics. I would wave and smile, uttering simple greetings that I had learned, and we would move on.

The rising sun beat down, having increased in intensity throughout the morning. At first it was comfortable, but soon it became unpleasant. By lunchtime, it was nearing 100 degrees. We would head to the trucks and drive back to our camp on the edge of the desert to sit out the heat of the day.

Again, I would stand outside my shack, situated on a hill, and watch as the sun set over the horizon, taking with it the heat of the day. As cool air prevailed, I trained on molded rock climbing grips that I'd hung from the rafters.

We repeated this every day for 10 weeks.

I finished the job lean and strong with a flush bank account and an empty duffel bag, having left everything I could with my team in Eritrea, hoping these items would ease their way of life. At the time, my life was devoid of obligations, so I decided to head to the mountains. I told my boss I would send him a note when I was looking for more work. Being supportive of my climbing career, he didn't mind giving me time off between contracts.

The measurements we had taken were translated into a map showing the gravitation fields of the area. They were composed with a level of precision high enough that our clients could see any anomalies of stronger gravity that might represent a place where high-density material may lie under the ground. In the case of western Eritrea, it was hoped that this represented gold deposits.

This hope was supported by another part of team—our geophysicists—who had quite literally struck gold a few years before in a nearby part of the country. It had been one of the largest gold discoveries in recent history, representing billions of dollars in potential revenue. This had been cause for immense excitement, as it meant that we would have far more work in front of us. More importantly, it meant that the country of Eritrea had an opportunity to break out of the vicious cycle of poverty and war. As we walked through the desert, I had looked to the men working with me and hoped their future would improve.

With this optimistic view on the impacts of my work in geophysics, I had continued to work—when not on expeditions—running surveys around the globe, from winters in the northern reaches of Canada to summers at other locations along the African Rift Valley. The jobs were consistently fast and loose, described by one of my colleagues as "cowboy."

I worked hard so that I could climb, making plenty of money to cover the expenses of expeditions and tuck a percentage away for the future. I was leaning into Kaj's advice, keeping my choices about climbing in my own court. The brands I was working with as a sponsored athlete had the ability to use my stories, but the decisions about where I went and how I climbed were all mine. For a young man hellbent on exploring the mountains of the world, it was the perfect job.

But this changed. Just after my knee surgery for the injury sustained in the Revelations, four years after departing Eritrea, I got an update on the project there. The Bisha Mine that had resulted from the mapping we had done had not been a driver of opportunity and global equality. Instead, it had led to allegations of forced labor, slavery, and torture. This had taken place alongside a mass exodus of hundreds of thousands of people from the small country of six million in the Horn of Africa, due to broader actions from the government, documented by Human Rights Watch, including large-scale massacres and summary executions. As a result, Eritrea had been accused by the international community of being a human rights pariah.

For me, it was a reality check. *Was I complicit in these crimes against humanity?*

I had tried to be kind to the small communities in which I had worked, but I had benefited immensely from the discovery of those resources—far more than the locals had. No longer could I ignore the impact of the work I was doing in an extractive industry. It created stability for me in the form of reliable income, but it was immoral and not sustainable for the world.

In the United States, Trayvon Martin had been murdered two years before, and I found myself comparing my actions to those that had resulted in the murder of Martin and countless other unarmed people of color. To me it all appeared interwoven—a global web of inequity in which I was favored and was not subject to violence as others were. I felt a need to take responsibility for how I benefited from this system to the detriment of others.

The contract work also required me to be absent from my life with Shannon for months at a time. After a slew of failed relationships, I knew that constantly being on an assignment or expedition was a sure-fire way to get dumped. Shannon was a partner worth investing in—I didn't want to lose her due to my constant travel.

The position that had initially seemed a perfect career, in which I could make money and have ample time for expeditions, was badly tainted. While I didn't have answers for how to solve the equity problems of the world, I knew ignoring them was a way to ensure they persisted. It was time to get out of my own world, to take responsibility, to take a bigger perspective: to keep learning and to find another way forward.

"Graham, you're climbing really well," said my friend Christian, "but if you want to continue to grow your career as an athlete, you should figure out how to create more content for your sponsors to use in the promotion of their brand—and yours."

We were sitting at a bistro table on the sidewalk outside a small coffee shop adjacent to the headquarters of Outdoor Research, one of my primary sponsors, in the SODO district of Seattle. Cars whipped by, the city hummed around us. The sun was out, and we were on our second cups of coffee. Christian was leading OR's marketing team, essentially making him my boss. He had also become a good friend.

"If you're the creator, not only can you charge your sponsors more money, but you can also control your own storytelling," he said.

We were having a conversation about finding a balance between sponsorship, my career, and my personal motivations for climbing. He knew I had spent most of the past five years organizing expeditions and running surveys. Maybe I could use those same skills in the creative space.

"Think about ways those stories about climbing can be an analog for other, dare I say, more important subjects," he said.

"That feels like it has a lot of potential," I replied. "A model in which I can maintain control over what I'm climbing while making more money from the work and trying to drive change for good? Wow."

After being named a finalist for the Piolets d'Or, I'd been offered the opportunity to create short films about climbing in Alaska for a European media group. I had produced and edited the shorts and enjoyed the work. My conversations from years before—in Seattle with Nick and in the Waddington with Forest—had helped inform my creative style. Throughout the process, I had watched the work of other filmmakers, seeking the secrets of effective storytelling. I felt like an aspiring painter, surrounded by the masterpieces of past generations, emulating those who came before me as I considered what my personal style of creation might look like.

Attempting to capture my love for the mountains, I wrote muscular soundbites about a personal drive for wild, hard terrain in the unknown corners of the world: "Massive remote and unclimbed mountains are what I seek. . . . Unknown corners, badass climbing, and rowdy adventures."

I laid them into the edit over wailing guitar riffs and video of steep granite mixed climbing. I sat back and looked at what I'd created. The final product was a short, raw, and electrifying video about exploring new terrain in Alaska, a fusion of a 1990s skateboarding video and an expedition journal. It had nothing to do with anything besides climbing, but I was delighted nonetheless.

"Keep it up, GZ," Christian said "This is a cool path for you to follow."

He and his team at OR had recently funded my first official creative assignment. Along with Forest and two fellow OR athletes—the talented couple Kyle Dempster and Jewell Lund—I returned to the Southern Alps of New Zealand. Together we collected stories and images. I now had the job of producing a film for the brand.

Kyle was a broad-shouldered, muscular young man. Only a few years older than me, he owned a coffee shop in Salt Lake City and was known by his climbing partners as the "Silverback Gorilla." The name came from his strength and grit in the mountains, as well as his immense experience within them.

He had taken a number of trips to the Greater Ranges, where he had done some amazing things. Early on, he had truly taken it to the edge when he attempted to solo a 22,000-foot wedge of granite in the Karakoram. Later, his explorations along the border of China and Kyrgyzstan had resulted in a series of amazing ascents. More recently, he had teamed up with Hayden Kennedy, with whom I had traveled to Nepal many years before. They'd found themselves perfectly matched and had forged a cutting-edge climbing alliance, both on granite walls in North America and on unclaimed giants in the Karakoram.

I badly wanted to be a peer of Kyle's. When I looked at the climbing he was completing, I saw the climbing I wanted to do.

Jewell was athletic and had an infectious laugh. She was an academic studying glaciology, and most of our conversations revolved around her groundbreaking work on the glaciers of the Karakoram. Behind her kind attitude and academic leanings, she was one of a handful of American women pushing the envelope of alpine climbing. She primarily teamed up with other women, and together they were taking trips to Alaska with an eye for new routes and hard repeats. With our mutual friend Chantel Astorga she had repeated testpiece climbs on both Mount Huntington and the massive south face of Denali. The two of them were leading the charge of women smashing the glass ceiling of American mountain climbing. Along with many others in our community, I stood in awe of what Jewell was accomplishing.

Forest and I shot video and looked for the story that we might tell about our journey. We ducked in and out of storms, sneaking in summits and walls. We enjoyed the freedom provided by being based out of a van, on the back of which we had placed a giant OR sticker. But the story we wanted to tell was not one of a group of privileged young folks running wild in New Zealand. We were looking for something deeper, something more meaningful.

As we traveled through the hills of the South Island, I relished being in the mountains that had taught me so much about climbing. And I could not help but notice the changes that were taking place. The glacial termini were pulling back and the lateral moraines were more exposed. These massive features that defined the peaks were disappearing, and I was left with a feeling of hopelessness that, in the moment, I needed to tuck away in lieu of more urgent tasks.

I considered the story that we could tell and thought back to Christian's comment about creating something larger than climbing. I found myself drawn to this story of the planet's changing climate—what had been known as global warming but was then becoming known as the climate crisis. From my years studying geography in university, I knew that it was real—and I knew the fault lay in humanity's hands. I was also aware that the changes were most dramatic in the high-altitude and high-latitude parts of the world, the places where I was spending much of my time. I wanted to work on a story that addressed the changing climate, but as I looked at those shrinking glaciers, I knew how to describe the change but not how to tell the story. I still had a lot to learn.

As I looked for a story to tell, I could also see changes within myself, changes in how I approached the mountains and how I climbed within them. I was a better climber, but I was also a smarter and safer climber. The progression toward safety and skill was evident with every move I made over the terrain. But I had been challenged to think less about my story and to look for the stories of others, so I tried to stay behind the camera and observe what was unfolding.

When I looked, the story was right in front of me. It was not the landscape, or my personal ego. The story I saw emerging was Kyle and Jewell: a couple, deeply in love, both with each other and with the exploration of steep new terrain in the mountains. For me, their love, forged in the high hills, represented a blending of the two most powerful forms of partnership I had experienced in life. I wanted to know more and to help them share it with the world.

As a team of four, we ascended the technically moderate north-west ridge of Mount Aspiring toward its summit. We scrambled over rock outcroppings and sections of steep snow as the exposure fell away beneath us. The clouds roiled as we watched the South Island emerge. Steep walls of rock and ice gave way to plateaus of glaciers that rolled into an expanse of forested valleys and open river plains. As we climbed, Forest took photos and video while I helped him stay safe as he positioned himself for the best frames. Meanwhile, Jewell and Kyle calmly took in the exposure while chatting about their work, their climbing, and their plans for the future. They were at home in the environment and with each other.

Later, in the southwestern corner of the South Island, we made our way up a sheer granite wall via a local testpiece climb. It was a route known for challenging sequences of climbing that were oftentimes far above the last piece of protection. We climbed as two rope teams. I led first, fixing the rope for Forest so that he could shoot Kyle and Jewell as they climbed below.

Sitting at each belay on the 750-foot route, I watched them communicate clearly and concisely as they climbed below us. The weather was sublime. They were in sync on the mountain. They were also clearly having fun. So was I.

As we reached the top of the wall, clouds started to blow in off the Southern Ocean and it started to rain. We climbed delicately through the final pitches to the summit, making sure not to slip off the now wet holds. This slowed us down, and by the time we summited, it was nearly dark.

The descent from the top of the wall followed a ridge down from the summit; at the bottom, we reached the route we had taken on the approach. From this point we had planned to follow our route back to the valley below and out to the road. But the slabs of rock that had been simple to navigate on the way up were now running with water, and in the clouds and dark we could see only 10 feet in any direction.

For hours we wandered on the endless slabs looking for the route back to the valley floor, but we were consistently foiled by steep terrain and rivulets of water streaking down the granite. Around two in the morning, we stopped, deciding that it would be safer to wait for daylight. Under an overhang of rock, we huddled on two small ledges—Kyle and Jewell on one, Forest and me on the other. They pulled out an emergency blanket. Forest and I crawled into a shared jacket.

As we sat shivering on the small ledge of rock, Forest and I listened to Jewell and Kyle laughing at the situation from under the thin film of their foil blanket. Even in this wild and uncomfortable space, they were enjoying each other's company.

The next morning, in the light of day, we were able to find our way back to the road, and after an hour of walking, were drinking freshly brewed coffee. As we sat warming ourselves with the hot liquid, we laughed at the absurdity of the night before. I had fallen for their story: two high-end alpinists in love with each other and the mountains in which they thrive.

Back home in the United States, I began editing, and the story came together slowly. I looked for moments in which they talked about their relationship and how it intersected with their passion for the mountains. How they made it happen emerged through examples of their support of each other—both when tied in together and when off on separate expeditions. It formed into a simple plotline and became a short film titled *Five Ways to Love in the Mountains*.

Looking back, I can see that while I was directing a film about two of my friends, I was also telling a story about what I had learned from them. Many of the items I listed—like "Be stoked on each other's adventures" and "Make the most of the time that you have together"—were things I was working to build into my relationship with Shannon in an effort to solidify our partnership.

Having now been together for two years, we were working hard to support each other in our respective sports, and it seemed to be working. I was gaining international recognition as an alpinist and, in 2014, Shannon had won her second world championship in Ultimate Frisbee. And things were continuing to develop.

After her second time winning on the global stage, this time in the mountains of northern Italy, Shannon had decided to retire from Frisbee in order to pursue her career. This allowed us to look for places to live other than Seattle. And due to its proximity to climbing, friends, mountains, and family, we chose the growing city of Bend, Oregon. Situated in the wild expanses of Central Oregon, among the cinder cones of ancient volcanoes and surrounded by juniper forests, it was a place where we had room to think, room to move, and room to grow.

By the time I was working through the final edits of the film from New Zealand, we were living in a rented space in Bend and learning about each other and our new environment. Bend was full of opportunity for us both. I could become a better climber, while Shannon was seeking full-time employment. We were working in concert, attempting to create the kind of life we wanted to lead. When we were in sync, not only was it effective, it was fun.

It was, of course, not that simple. Being part of the core climbing community is to always know at least one person at any given moment who is out pushing their limits in the mountains. With more stability in my life, I had more time to train and prepare for larger expeditions. I also had more settled moments in which to consider my friends and climbing partners. These concerns about the safety of friends were oftentimes easy to push aside, but they were ever present.

Kyle and our friend Scott Adamson were in Pakistan, trying to make the first ascent of the north face of Baintha Brakk II (also known as Ogre II), a truly groundbreaking wall that shoots off the Choktoi Glacier and rises at a very steep angle for 4,600 feet to the summit ridge. This was their second time attempting the series of ramps and smears that connected, barely, to the top of the wall. The first time they had tried the route, the year before, it had nearly ended in disaster when Scott took a large fall, high on the wall, that resulted in a broken leg. Then, while they were self-rescuing off the wall and were nearly to the ground, an anchor failed, sending them both tumbling to the glacier below. Luckily, neither of them sustained further injuries in the second fall, and they made it to base camp safely.

Now, a year later, they had headed back.

▲

IN CLIMBING PARTNERSHIPS, there is oftentimes a yin and yang in how much boldness the partners bring to the table. One partner is more willing to take the sharp end of the rope on the hardest pitches, to lead above the gear and push into the unknown. On my expeditions, I have, at times, been on both sides of the equation, depending on the demands and style of the climbing. Some days the nuance of this risk-and-reward calculation results in audacity, and some days I am happy to hand off the lead. But there are a few climbers who are able to consistently hold that edge and quest into the unknown, pitch after pitch and climb after climb.

Both Scott and Kyle were this type of climber—not only exceptionally talented but also consistently bold. Because of this, I looked up to both of them. Because of this, I was both excited and concerned about them tying in together in the big mountains. The things they could accomplish were outstanding, but at times I found the risks they were willing to take unfathomable.

It was the third week of August in 2016 when I got a call from a friend. "Hey, Graham, do you have a few minutes? We might have a problem in Pakistan." While on the wall, Kyle and Scott had disappeared into a storm.

When friends are lost in the mountains, grief is a strange process. It comes on slowly, due to the slim chance that they may emerge from the wreckage of the expedition. There are a few of these tales in the history of climbing, when a climber, assumed dead, miraculously crawls out of the grasp of the mountains. These are stories that we, as a community, hold dear. They give us hope when it otherwise seems that all is lost.

Kyle and Scott had started the climb on the 21st of August, with plans to return to base camp on the 26th, but alarms had sounded in our core crew of alpinists when a large storm blew in on the 23rd. We hoped that the tenacity and drive of these men, the bold nature that had allowed them to survive on the edge, would get them down safe.

As news of their disappearance reached a broader audience, money poured in to help with search efforts. Helicopters from the Pakistan military were hired to scour the area between storm cycles. Teams in nearby base camps shifted from their chosen objectives to that of finding their lost friends. But, by September 3, when no sign of them had been found, the search was called off. Only after all that effort and time could it be assumed that they had in fact perished.

After nearly two weeks of hoping that they would emerge, I was emotionally exhausted.

I worried about Jewell, knowing that her sense of loss was orders of magnitude greater than my own.

I learned that there would be a memorial a few weeks later, but it conflicted with my own expedition plans. I told myself Kyle would have wanted me to go climbing. *He died doing what he loved; this is the best way to honor him.* I ignored the fact that Shannon very likely did not want me to head into the mountains at all. I skipped the memorial and headed to the hills.

There are very few things that I regret in my life. Skipping Kyle's memorial is one of them. My rationalization was bullshit. Kyle's last thoughts were not about his love for climbing. Shannon and my community should have been my priority. Going on another expedition was selfish.

That fall, the film about Kyle and Jewell climbing in New Zealand made its premiere at an adventure film festival called 5Point, in Carbondale, Colorado. It was run by Hayden Kennedy's mother, Julie.

Before the screening, I sat with Hayden on the edge of the door of his van, in the parking lot outside the venue. He and Kyle had been close, and he was devastated by the loss to the point of being angry at Kyle for making bad decisions. He had gone to the memorial and had the grace not to ask where I had been. I didn't tell him about the expedition, knowing that it didn't matter. We shared few words. Neither of us had much to say.

In the original cut, the final slide in the film had stated, "As of the release of this film, Kyle and Jewell continue to crush in the mountains, and on each other." I'd added a slide at the end stating that the film was in memory of Kyle, who had been lost in the mountains.

I sat next to Shannon, among a small sea of people in the dark theater, as the film played. We held hands. As we did, I wondered if a balance between our love, a stable life, and climbing in the big mountains was possible. And if it *was* possible, what was the point? Where did all the effort I was pouring into mountain climbing go? Was it wasted? Was I wasting my time?

Later that day, I stood outside the theater holding a drink in the cool fall Colorado sunshine and chatting with a new friend. Brody Leven was a professional skier hell-bent on combining human-powered adventure with remarkable first descents on skis. In a world where the high carbon cost of helicopter-assisted skiing remained a mainstay, he had given up even getting on a ski lift, preferring instead to use the power of his legs to ascend the peaks he skied. And the skiing he was taking on was incredible.

In Alaska the following spring, I would stand mere feet away as he dropped into a thin 3,000-foot sliver of snow-covered ice called *Ham and Eggs*, a well-known technical climbing route. Brody was calm and under control, making turns on the 50-degree terrain in which a fall would undoubtedly be fatal. I was both terrified by and amazed at his skill and grace under pressure.

But there, at the film festival, I didn't feel like talking about climbing and skiing. Keen to move the conversation to other subjects, I asked about another part of Brody's work—his political advocacy around climate change.

I knew he had used his experience in the mountains as a tool to drive climate policy—both within his community and when talking to politicians—and I peppered him with questions.

"Is it advocacy? Activism? Is there a difference?"

"How do you balance that against all the travel you need to do for work?"

"Listen, man," Brody said, "your curiosity, alongside your knowledge about earth science, leads me to believe you might be interested in getting involved. How about I introduce you to Barbara, one of the leaders at Protect Our Winters, the org through which I do most of this work. She's right over there." He pointed toward a woman who sat chatting with a small group of people nearby.

"Hey, Barbara," Brody said, butting in on her conversation. "This is Graham. He's a badass alpinist with a background in glacier science and is curious about working with POW. You two should chat."

"Yes, please!" she said, smiling at me. "Do you have a minute right now?"

I sat down next to her and asked about the work that POW did. She explained their goal was to activate athletes to be political advocates for policy around our changing climate. They had mostly been operating in the snowboard and ski space but were keen to work with a broader range of outdoor activities, climbing included.

"But how can I do this work if I am burning carbon while heading off to wild, far-flung places to climb?" I asked.

She explained their program was about giving athletes a way to use our adventures and the changes we were seeing in the mountains to drive needed policy. Had I seen any changes?

I thought back to those glaciers in New Zealand and the academic work I had done in glaciology. My answer was clear: Yes.

"Well, do you want to use those stories you collect every year when you go on expeditions to help fix this problem?"

I did.

8

The Karakoram

When I was 10 years old, my grandfather gave me a subscription to *National Geographic*, and each month I eagerly looked forward to its arrival. I would immerse myself in each issue—still too young to understand everything in it. I focused instead on the images and the maps. Each month I was transported to the unimaginably lush rainforests of Brazil, the jagged karst landscapes of China, or the frigid expanses of the Antarctic. My world expanded as I imagined the places, the people, and the discoveries and stories collected within the pages.

The cover of the April 1996 issue featured a man hanging by his fingertips from a rock wall, far above a jagged range of peaks and massive glaciers. In the article, penned by climber Todd Skinner, I read that the man's name was Bobby Model and he was climbing on a peak named Trango Tower in the Karakoram Range of Pakistan. I was entranced.

I had no idea that I was looking at photos of the cutting edge of alpinism. Those rock climbers were free climbing the route, using only their hands and feet to make upward progress on the rock; the ropes and protection were there only to catch falls. But the images of the

Karakoram, among the highest and most jagged peaks on the planet, stayed with me. As I progressed in the practice of mountain climbing, those memories rose back to the surface. To become the climber I wanted to be, I would need to go to the Karakoram.

This turned out to be far harder than I had anticipated. All the expeditions I had undertaken as a young climber had been relatively simple to plan: call the pilot in Alaska or the fixer in Kyrgyzstan, tell them where we wanted to go, wire them money, and buy an airplane ticket. In the case of Patagonia, all we had to do was show up. But gaining access to the Islamic Republic of Pakistan was challenging, let alone convincing the government that they should allow us to go to the mountains along their field of battle with India as they fought to control the former Khanate of Kashmir and the mountains to its north.

In 2012, the highly productive expedition to the Waddington Range with Blake and Scott had, in fact, been a last-minute backup plan when our visas to Pakistan failed to come through. We had sent all the appropriate information to the consulate in Los Angeles and called them repeatedly, asking for an update. Our original plans had been to attempt the second ascent of a peak named Tahu Ratum in the remote Hispar region of the Karakoram. But without visas, we were not able to go, so we pivoted our sights to the walls in the Waddington.

In 2013, our visas arrived without a hitch. But our plans were shut down when, a few weeks before our intended departure, militants showed up in the base camp for Nanga Parbat and murdered 11 people. Ten of them were foreign climbers. It became impossible to justify the expedition. Blake stayed home. Scott and I went to Alaska.

It was clear that the political situation in Pakistan was unstable and, without any experience in the range, I didn't feel that I could rationalize traveling to that part of the world.

"It doesn't fit into the 100-year plan," I told Shannon. "The only way it would make sense is if one of the sages of the range, someone like Steve Swenson, invited me on a trip."

Steve had more than 15 expeditions to the Pakistani and Indian Karakoram to his credit. Not only was he one of the most experienced

Karakoram climbers, but he was also one of the most successful, having made ascents of cutting-edge climbs from the infamous north ridge of K2 in 1990 to the remote and wild Saser Kangri II in 2011.

I had met Steve a number of times over the years, at climbing events and at crags, but I didn't know if he'd noticed me beyond offering kind encouragement. Therefore, it came as a surprise when I received an email from him: "I'm putting together a trip to Pakistan for 2015, and I'm wondering if you and a partner of yours might be interested."

Steve proposed that we attempt the south face of a peak called K6. Scott and I, having given up on going to Pakistan, planned to head into the Nepali Himal, but we couldn't pass up the opportunity to climb in the Karakoram with someone who knew its peaks so well.

A few weeks later, after a flurry of email exchanges, we met up in person. I told Steve I was all in, but I needed him to provide me with the information that would allow me to prove to Shannon that it was not a terrible idea. Without missing a beat, he shared the social and political dynamics that he felt made a strong case for our expedition being safe. The next day, he followed up with supporting evidence, primarily from the *New York Times*. I was impressed. So was Shannon.

Steve took on planning the expedition with a practiced tenacity. I tried to help when I could but generally spent far more time learning about his processes for running an expedition. One day, while we were looking over a table of maps and photographs, me drinking coffee, Steve with a cup of tea, he told me about his friend Haji Ghulam Rasool, a community leader in the small mountain village of Hushe. They had been going on expeditions together, with Steve climbing and Rasool cooking, since the mid-1980s. Steve confided in me that while he was very excited to see the mountains and climb, he was just as excited to see his dear friend.

It was clear I was in for far more than just a climbing trip.

▲

ON JULY 10, we reached our small base camp, tucked into a clutch of boulders on the grassy slope above the glacier, under a constant downpour. I fumbled through stacks of bills with numb hands, paying our 44 porters and shaking their hands before they left for the warmth of their homes deep in the valley below. As we passed through their villages of Kande and Hushe, local men told us of past decades when many expeditions visited the region and portering work had been easier to find. It was hard labor, and at times dangerous, but it provided a seasonal income to supplement their farming. In recent years, the numbers of foreign climbers and trekkers had greatly diminished, kept away by fears of violence in other parts of the country.

Carrying 55-pound loads and wearing simple wool clothes, the porters moved quickly up the approach to our base camp. We chatted about life in the Hushe Valley: the long, frigid winters; the common chest ailments; the homemade skis the children enjoyed so much that the local teacher had trouble keeping them in school during the snowy months; the jagged beauty of the surrounding mountains. Tell your climbing friends back home how wonderful Hushe is, they urged me, before they descended below the clouds.

Through the mist, the shadows of high peaks loomed over the grassy hillside. Above the pitter-patter of the rain, I could hear Rasool speaking Urdu in an excited voice to his son-in-law, Nadeem, while they expertly built platforms and constructed tents. As the first part of Rasool's name indicated, he was one of the few villagers who had participated in the hajj, the pilgrimage to distant Mecca. When I arrived, Rasool greeted me as he would have family.

"Steve is like a brother," he told me. "If you are friends, then so are we." He then pulled me into a big hug. Rasool and Steve had gone on many trips together throughout the Karakoram, accumulating an intimate knowledge of the range. Now we were all in base camp together for two months of climbing.

The clouds cleared two days after we reached base camp. Up valley, the southern aspects of K6 gleamed with a wild energy, both terrifying and alluring. Beyond the ridgeline to the east, the top of the south pillar and the untrodden summit of K6 Central rose above the Lachit Glacier. There was another unclimbed tower nearby, called Changi, more than 1,500 feet lower than K6. From an advanced base camp on the Lachit, we intended to attempt both peaks. Scott, Steve, and I took turns peering through our monocular, trying to discern the features we'd studied so long on paper. Gradually, imagined landscapes transformed into real mountains: dense contour lines turned into steep ridges and faces; elusive dreams solidified into tangible forms of rock and snow.

Fifteen years of climbing had taught me which aspects I liked the best. I was drawn to objectives that were large, steep, and unclimbed. I liked being in areas where I rarely saw other teams, where my partners and I were secluded in the wilds, able to make our own decisions based on survival, away from the influence of other opinions and egos.

I had learned to stay away from couloirs and other concavities where falling debris collected. Instead, I trended toward arêtes and buttresses, convexities that had less overhead hazard. I also discovered that this was where the steepest and best climbing was to be found. And snow was a hazard; any time I could stay away from it was a good thing.

As I looked up at those Karakoram peaks, I realized this range was the place I would find my personal ultimate climbs. The faces were huge and many of them remained unclimbed. Many of the peaks themselves remained unclimbed. And it was an arid range, oftentimes lacking in the snow that plagued other big mountains around the world. The rock was primarily granite, solid and steep—in my opinion, the best for climbing.

My early inspiration from the cover of *National Geographic* had been on point. The Karakoram was the place for me.

On July 23, I sat on a rocky outcrop in the midst of a steep icefall below Changi Tower. One by one, I sketched in my journal the succession of ridgelines that faded into the vanishing point. As the sunset spread deep crimsons and purples over the horizon, I imagined all the journeys that had taken place in the sea of mountains before me: the first people who ventured up the valleys seeking pastures; the early climbers who strove to reach the wild summits.

Eight days earlier, Steve, Scott, and I had started moving our equipment over a small col to establish an advanced base camp at the head of the Lachit. Murky, low clouds insulated the glaciers. Deep, wet snow sucked us downward. At times, the sun emerged, igniting the walls with dazzling light. Daggers of water ice glittered.

As we rested outside our tent in advanced base camp, a huge serac collapsed on the south side of K6, adjacent to the central pillar. Tons of ice crashed down the flank of the mountain, generating an ever-larger cloud of white and scouring the lower 2,000 feet of the face. Once the cloud touched down a half mile away, we realized it was going to surge toward us. We dove into our tent before the barrage of wind and crystals hit. When the dusting had passed, we clambered out into the chilled air. After a short discussion, we decided the K6 route that we'd traveled halfway around the world to climb was simply too dangerous to warrant an attempt. A calm fell over us.

Scott and I stood looking at the buttress, our eyes still tracing our imagined lines through the ice runnels to the summit. Steve slipped back into the tent and focused on his journal. I pushed the idea of running under seracs from my mind and turned my thoughts to the north ridge of Changi instead.

In 2010, another team had attempted the first ascent of Changi Tower, climbing to just above a notch now known as the Polish Col. Above that point, the north ridge sweeps upward in an arc, transforming quickly from steep snow to dark, ice-streaked stone. Higher still, barren rock rears to a small summit. It looked exactly like what we sought: a technical route with little objective hazard. We set up our bivy a mile away from advanced base camp, on a small point of rock within a steep jumble of flowing ice.

In the cold of morning, when the sun lit our icefall again, we moved rapidly through the final sections of crumbling glacier to a glacial bowl. Scott and I knelt in the snow next to Steve while he organized gear to leave in a cache. I looked at the sky: its hues had deepened to the grays of another incoming storm. We set up a tent, placed equipment and food inside, and then descended, hoping to arrive in advanced base camp before the darkness and the snow fell.

Back in base camp, on the first day of August, I moved my hands across the lip of a boulder, one heel hooked in a shallow scoop. Holding my body tight, I grabbed a small edge, released my feet, and swung them left to a small foothold, pushing off it as I surmounted the final swath of overhanging stone. Sitting on top, I felt the stone with my hand, and I thought of the path the boulder had traveled, uplifted from deep inside the earth and then tumbled down again from one of the surrounding mountainsides. I gazed up, trying to guess where it came from. To the south, storm clouds were once again building toward a torrent of rain and lightning, as they had for the past six days.

Rasool hollered, "Super soup!" from the cook tent. I downclimbed and walked back to our mess tent.

Bluegrass hummed from the speaker on the table. Scott sat in his oversized puffy jacket, leaning over his book, a tepid cup of tea next to him. "Hey, man, how's it looking out there?" he asked.

"Our usual afternoon thunderstorm," I replied.

He pulled up the forecast on the sat phone. "Clear days with electrical storms in the evening. This pattern has to break down at some point, correct?"

I grumbled, "I sure fucking hope so." I sat down across the table and started writing in my expedition journal.

A few minutes later, Steve and Rasool ducked through the flap of the tent door. Rasool said he was worried that we might run out of food. He apologized, as if the weather were his responsibility.

"There is no way any of us could have known that we'd be spending this much time in base camp," Steve assured him. Rasool's tense face relaxed.

"Well then, sirs, what would you like for dinner?"

Steve looked at me. "Tonight's your choice, G."

"In that case, dhal bhat," I said, smiling. The traditional lentil soup served over steamed rice was almost always my choice for dinner.

Rasool gave a chef's kiss before shuffling out of the mess tent.

Steve sat down and gave us his daily update on what he was reading. I told them I had talked to Shannon on the sat phone; all was well on the home front.

"Seems like those sensitive guy points are paying off," Steve teased.

Over the course of the expedition, Steve had been sharing with us small bits of beta about how he had managed to pursue a successful career as an engineer while being an excellent partner to his wife, a great dad, and one of the world's foremost Karakoram alpinists.

The sensitive guy points he mentioned were a metric for ensuring that one spends enough time at home being a good partner. You gained sensitive guy points by being a present, loving, and accountable partner; you spent them by doing things that were more selfish—in our case, going climbing. The key was to treat it like a bank account that needed to be kept balanced; any large withdrawal needed to be preceded by a series of small, consistent deposits.

My journal from the expedition was packed with little sections marked "Steve Beta." These sections included advice on how to run an expedition:

Very clearly designate jobs to all expedition members, including treasurer, leader . . .

Stay calm, the pace here is different, you need to be okay with it.

There was also advice doled out as we talked about life outside of climbing in the Karakoram:

Do what you need to in order to own your home. It will require you to work more and climb less, but it will give you the foundation needed to go on big trips like this.

Put the time in to build a career that both makes you enough money and provides you enough time to support both climbing and your partnership with Shannon.

Steve and I were of the same mind about climbing. We both loved a day rock climbing at the local cliff, but these wild adventures to far-flung objectives were what truly sang to our souls. His advice for me was consistently to build a foundation of home, relationship, and career. A foundation from which I could launch into the big mountains.

It was a different vision from the all-or-nothing pathway that dominated the cultural airwaves of our climbing community. I found it resonated with what I wanted.

That night, I sat reading a book on climate change in my tent. The pile of books and articles I had brought into the range had been recommendations from Brody and the team at POW. I was attempting to connect the dots between my academic background and the communication and storytelling skills needed to drive climate action.

Reading books with titles like *This Changes Everything: Capitalism vs. the Climate, The End of Western Civilization,* and *The Sixth Extinction* was proving informative and inspiring but also terrifying. Sitting in my tent thousands of miles from home, a distance that I'd covered via carbon-expensive flights, I felt worse than impotent. Fortunately, the towering mountains surrounding our camp provided a quiet space in which I could meditate on these problems rather than just let them simmer in the back of my mind. In my journal, I recorded notes:

Being here feels important to my personal progression as an athlete, but I need to find a way to leverage these trips to work on climate.

And a few pages later:

Rasool and his family have a tiny carbon footprint but are on the front lines of climate impact. Can I use his story to drive change?

The mountains surrounding our base camp—indeed the entire range—were new to me. Unlike Alaska or New Zealand, where I had many years of experience and could recognize change, I had no frame of reference for the Karakoram. I had learned from Jewell that the range was being subject to what was becoming known as the "Karakoram Anomaly." In contrast to the retreat of glaciers in nearly every other range in the world, scientists were finding what they called "anomalous growth" in the Karakoram glaciers, associated with increased monsoons and the amount of rock present on top of the ice. It was fascinating but I was overwhelmed. I put my book down and pushed away the journal.

Years of expeditions had taught me patience. Either the weather would clear or it wouldn't. In the meantime, I could enjoy the simple meditation of bouldering, stretching, eating, and sleeping, my mind concentrated only on the present.

It also gave me an expansive state of mind from which I could evaluate the rest of my life—what was working and what was not. I noted in my journal that I should consider running my own company so I could build a career while giving myself the time to get away on expeditions. I also wrote about Shannon. Our partnership was thriving. Was it time to ask her to marry me? How was I supposed to know?

Six days later, Scott, Steve, and I were once again headed toward Changi Tower, wading slowly through deep, wet snow. Soft flakes began to fall as we climbed the ridgeline separating the Nangmah Valley from the Lachit Glacier. As we crested the ridge, clouds swirled around the tower, interspersed with flashes of brilliant blue sky. We kept going; the forecast promised four days of good weather.

The next day, I stood outside the tent under cloudless skies with Steve and Scott. We watched the mountains around us shed fresh layers of snow. As the sun moved across the sky, it warmed new aspects, continually setting off small avalanches. But with each release, the potential paths on the mountains became a little safer. "Well, guys," Steve said, "we've now been moving food and equipment around for weeks. It's finally time to go climbing." A wry expression spread across his suntanned face.

Two days later, we were finally on the peak itself. As I dragged one pick through a mush of snow, I felt it latch onto something. I looked down at the piton I'd placed behind a hollow flake and then I used my shoulder to bounce-test the hidden edge. With my body rigid and my breath held, I closed my eyes. I felt my existence shrink to a single point as I opened my eyes, placed my faith in an axe tip hooked on a fringe of rock, and moved up.

Soon I swung the other axe into a vein of soft ice and relaxed at the feeling of a sound placement. After I built a belay and fixed the ropes, I leaned back in my harness. To the east, the peaks of the Saltoro Group straddled the Actual Ground Position Line between Pakistan and India, their summits still closed to climbers. I tried to visualize how Changi Tower's wedge of stone might appear to soldiers along the distant ridgetops in some of the highest battlefields of the world.

The heavens opened into a brilliant blue, the horizon expanding to encompass ridges upon ridges of unknown mountains. Soon I was grasping golden huecos and placing cams in deep cracks. At the base of the rockband, Steve began work on a bivy ledge, while Scott and I continued following the granite edges and scoops through the corners and faces above. Ice filled some of the fissures and snow lined the ledges, but the rock remained sound, and when we reached a snow ramp that led to the final headwalls, we let out whoops. The summit appeared close, and the sky was still clear.

Back at the ledge, Steve had used a large swath of nylon tarp to harness snow and ice into a ledge—an ingenious technique one of his partners, Mark Richey, had developed, and a reminder of how much I had to learn from such great alpinists. Scott looked around him with an air of confidence. "I think we should leave the tent here and push to the summit tomorrow," he said. I agreed, finding it easy to join his exuberance.

"Guys, it might take us longer to get to the summit than you think," Steve replied. His tone sounded well practiced from many conversations with younger climbers, firm and certain yet gentle. "We still have a ways to go."

Steve explained that he didn't want to have to retreat in good weather simply because we didn't have the equipment to spend another night out. Depending on how much we planned to carry, the topography above us seemed to either lengthen or shrink, but Scott was confident that we could make it to the top. In the end, we found a middle ground, deciding that we'd leave the tent on the ledge but bring one sleeping bag and the stove, a balance of speed and security that would—with luck—take us through to the untouched apex of the tower.

The next day, I watched in awe as Scott acted on his statement of the night before. He climbed quickly through a wide-open dihedral, switching between boots and rock shoes, between stemming on edges and standing in slings. Steve and I sat at the belay under a small roof as small pieces of ice and rock flew by. A dark roof capped the top of the corner and sealed off our view of the terrain above. *Maybe we'd reached an impasse*, I thought. To my surprise, Scott traversed rapidly under the roof and pulled over a ledge, disappearing from sight. A few minutes later, he called out, "Rope fixed!"

Light snow drifted around us. A gray haze filled the sky. "I'm glad we're moving so fast," Steve said in a quiet voice. After jugging the bottom section of the pitch, I lowered out from a nut in the corner to clear the roof. To its side, I saw that Scott had found a series of fortuitously placed orange huecos and gray edges, the result of an ancient injection of younger, darker rock into the light granite of the tower. I remembered all the times in my past when the mountains had offered precisely what I needed for forward progress: a small edge on which to stand in the middle of a crux, a hidden couloir through a blank section of stone, a sense of pattern to the chaos of natural forms. When I reached the small cave where Scott had built an anchor, he was looking out at the mountains on the horizon while lounging and methodically eating an energy bar. Up until this point, he had short-fixed many of the pitches, but having exhausted the rack on the pitch below, he had waited for me to arrive. "I think we might just get up this thing," he said with a stubbly grin.

After two more pitches of golden granite and soft snow, I was next to the rocky summit block with Scott. The snow had stopped. High peaks poked through a thin layer of clouds. The sun dove toward the horizon. Ten minutes later, Steve reached the anchor in complete darkness.

The summit had room for only one person so we each made the last couple of moves individually and stood on the summit on our own. The moon was small, and a light haze of clouds blocked the starlight. As I stood on the wedge of stone, I looked out into the deep darkness of the Karakoram. Despite the expansive view, civilization was nowhere to be seen. The light from my headlamp disappeared into the atmosphere, absorbed into the void. At the apex of Changi Tower, I stood staring into nothing, and through the clag of my fatigue it felt both alarmingly empty and enticingly full of potential. For a long, final moment, I stared into the infinite, a place where everything could either end or begin—uncomfortable but alluring at the same time. I blinked and shook my head, then downclimbed to Steve and Scott. I started drilling the first V-thread anchor and leading our descent into night.

We reached the bivy ledge just after 3:00 a.m. Snow fell lightly on our cloudy perch. Even our small tent felt luxurious. The tension in Steve's and Scott's faces had given way to hollow-cheeked fatigue.

"Great job today, guys," Steve said. He lay down and shut his eyes. Scott, his face already half-covered by his neck gaiter, beamed as he wiggled deeper into his sleeping bag.

"Thank you for getting us here," I replied, resting my head on the rope stacked at the front of the tent. A feeling of gratitude for my partners washed over me—the trust and faith we had in each other, what we could accomplish together—and I fell into a deep sleep.

Three days later, we walked the final few miles to base camp. As I trudged, exhausted, through the soupy snow, I kept looking back up at the tall buttresses that descended from the west summit of K6; below them, a narrow ridge wound to a notch, attainable from a snow and ice slope. The weight of the original mountain we'd hoped to climb still loomed above me.

Rasool greeted us with a bouquet of flowers delicately picked from the steep, green pastures around camp. As we recounted the tale to him and Nadeem, I realized how integral Steve had been on the ascent.

While he had not led a pitch on the climb, his team design and strategy had allowed Scott and me to attain the mountain's challenging pitches. Without the structure that he brought to the expedition, it is unlikely we would have even reached the mountain.

The next morning, as I sat at the breakfast table, I recorded more Steve beta in my journal.

If a partner is firing, let them lead.

Be strategic with your planning; have a clear idea of where you are trying to reach on any particular pitch or day of climbing.

Never neglect to bounce-test your rap anchor.

When I looked up from my notes, I saw Steve across the tent, drinking tea with Rasool. Steve's shoulders hunched a little with weariness, but his dark eyes shone in a way that made him seem, suddenly, much younger than his years.

While we were gone, Rasool had hired two porters from Hushe to walk up to base camp with more supplies, ensuring that we had plenty of food and fuel for the remainder of the trip. They also brought with them news from the village: the purchase of cows and the birth of baby goats, but also flooding from heavy rains. The same weather that had limited our climbing could, if it continued, have far more serious consequences for those who lived in the valleys. We were relieved to hear that while the road had washed out, there was no damage to the town or its inhabitants. I made another note in my journal with a star next to it:

Increased rainfall because of increased temperatures? Or just a highly dynamic alpine geography? Probably both? Research.

The far-flung land of Gilgit-Balistan—the northern region of Pakistan in which the high Karakoram resides—had for many years been a place I had studied and dreamed of, but it was now becoming real to me.

The hazard to communities from rainfall and floods from glacial recession was transforming from a global statistic, which I could view with emotional detachment, to something that was part of my lived experience. I now knew the faces and stories of those who would be harmed.

Similarly, the broader influence of European meddling in the region, which exemplified the strength, audacity, and utter disregard for humanity of the colonial-era British Empire, had become something I could see firsthand. While in Skardu, the town in Gilgit-Baltistan from which we launched our expedition, I spent an afternoon with the son of the family who had reigned over that region until the British had taken control during the Great Game era of the 19th century.

This man, introduced as a prince by our mutual friend, wore a feather in his traditional Balti hat. We sat in a small garden behind a hotel and ate fresh apricots while discussing the development of the area. He spoke Urdu (which my friends translated) and wore a scowl as he talked about the installation of the China–Pakistan Economic Corridor—a road that travels from the deepwater ports to the south and then up and over the Karakoram to China—and its influence on local economies. I wanted to be on his side, to support the communities of the region, but after generations of outsiders taking advantage, he clearly regarded me with skepticism.

It left me considering my impact. In Eritrea, I had inadvertently become part of a very negative international influence; in Pakistan, I needed to do better. Could I use my time to help beyond the cash injection inherent to our expedition? Could I do more?

Back in our base camp mess tent, Scott pulled up the latest forecast on the sat phone. "Fellas," he said, "we've got another window on its way. We might just get a chance to try K6 after all."

A day later, as we sat drinking tea in the dim light of the cook tent, Steve announced he'd decided not to join us on the second route. He felt he'd shared with us much of what he knew about the Karakoram and that he was excited to send us onto K6 on our own, to use what we'd learned in addition to our strength as young climbers. He said we'd recover more quickly than he would from Changi Tower, and we'd move faster without him.

He also said he was feeling satisfied; he didn't need to push his body through another hard ascent on this trip.

Scott sat quietly with his chin resting in his palm. I blinked and slowly sat up. I had gotten comfortable having Steve's advice always at our beck and call but was psyched to attempt the route, even without him. Scott said his feelings reflected mine. We both told Steve how much we appreciated the knowledge and experience he had shared and how excited we were to utilize what we had learned on K6.

Silently, I envied Steve's satisfaction and contentment; I still badly wanted more. Taking his advice, I began a dedicated regime of performing light recovery exercises, eating heavily, and napping often.

Five days later, Scott and I drank strong coffee as Steve and Rasool wished us well. The forecast called for four more days of clear weather before a deep low-pressure system would bring high winds and precipitation. We'd need to move with speed and confidence.

Scott and I left in the late evening under a stormy sky. The rocky path out of base camp was now familiar as we moved toward the mountain, still shrouded above us in swirling clouds and immense night.

We'd planned to keep going through the cool of dark, but the fog and the snow fell too thickly, so we bivied and started again at first light. By the time the sun hit the mountain, we were on the snow and ice face at the beginning of the route. Unroped, we took turns breaking trail as the surface melted in the heat. Sweat soaked my skin. Each time I glanced up, the crest of the ridge still appeared far away. Just after noon, I switched from frontpointing sideways along the flank of the ridge to walking straight ahead: the slope had become nearly horizontal.

Scott and I created a bivy ledge utilizing the tarp method Steve had taught us. We were up and moving by 3:00 a.m. White crystals sparkled in my headlamp beam. The angle of the snow reared up in the dark, suggesting steep buttresses ahead. As the sun rose, the geography expanded: to our right, ridges cascaded off the mountain, dripping with the wild swooping ice of seracs; to our left, Kapura South rose, massive and blunt. Above us, two large towers dominated the middle of our intended route. Could we move past them quickly enough to summit? From below they appeared compact and sheer, but we continued forward, hoping that a path would present itself. A series of snow ledges slowly materialized, traversing up and left along the western side of the walls, forming streaks of white against the dark, fractured granite. Once again, the mountain provided exactly what we needed.

Under a narrow gash in the gray-red granite, Scott stopped to build an anchor. We'd already climbed through several short cruxes, but the one ahead looked steeper than anything we'd faced so far: a small dagger dangling from an overhanging chimney.

I tapped carefully into the ice, pulled up, and placed a wire in a small crack. I set one frontpoint onto an edge and placed the other on an opposing wall, allowing me to release much of my weight onto my legs. I locked off on my right tool and swung into the top of the dagger where it was bonded to the rock. When my pick set, I committed one foot onto the hanging ice. Moving quickly, I hooked into a crack above the dagger and placed a cam in a small fissure. I took a deep breath and waited until my heartbeat calmed.

Soon, I was standing on a snowy terrace. Fifty feet below, Scott was gazing beyond the expanse of mountains to the west, immersed in private thoughts. I gave him a monkey call, reminiscent of our days in Yosemite. He hollered back. Ahead, the ledges continued diagonally up until they disappeared into a series of rocky ribs below a large ice face. I smiled at the shadows beneath us; the sun was low in the sky, the hour was still early.

Three hours later, I belayed Scott across the final 75 feet of undulating rock ribs to reach the ice sheet. I pulled off my jacket. We were now directly under the zenith of the sun. A scattering of snow lay over hard, solid ice. I set a rhythm of kicking hard with my now blunt crampons, silently repeating *precision, strength, patience* until I lost myself in the methodical pattern of movement, thought, and breath.

As the sun rolled slowly over the horizon, the angle of the slope we were climbing started to lessen again. The air cooled as evening approached. I could see a white ridgeline cresting off the top of the upper tower. I hoped we'd find a comfortable place to sleep.

The red hues of sunset began to fade from the snows. Scott, now out of view, traversed back and forth, looking for a place to rest. Finally, I heard a whoop and the rope came tight. I followed his steps in the dim light. He stood on a wide part of the ridge—a perfect bivy spot. Through the dusk, we could still see the way forward, a final 1,400 feet of rolling glacier ice. Over dinner, we came to the conclusion that we needed to start our descent by the next night to avoid the forecasted storm. We laughed as we quoted Steve Beta for reference, but I felt that our decisions had a new weight behind them, a glint of experience. Like Steve, we'd try to aim for both success and safety.

Our new plan gave us only one chance to make it to the top. Scott set the alarm for 5:00 a.m. I looked down toward the darkness of the valley below and thought of Rasool and Steve back at our base camp, far away and invisible somewhere in the dark. Perhaps they were looking for our lights, wondering about us, wishing us well.

The sky above was clear and stars began to dot the sky, spreading into the tangled iridescent mass of the Milky Way. I looked out at the universe and thought back to the sense of the infinite on top of Changi, only 10 days before. This expanse of starlight was another metaphor for the sense of endless possibilities spreading out before us. In that moment, tucked into my thin sleeping bag and wearing all my clothing for warmth with the summit of K6 West just above us, there was nowhere I would have rather been.

The next morning, I swore under my breath as I struggled through waist-deep snow. I turned to Scott, his eyes bleary and distant from days of hard climbing at altitude. I suggested that we might need to try a more circuitous but lower-angle route to the final summit ridge, passing through the disarray of seracs and crevasses. With a ragged voice, he agreed. I downclimbed and started traversing across the slope. His breaths heaved behind me. While his pace slowed, he didn't complain. I knew he was as driven to reach the summit as I was.

Near 23,000 feet, I crested onto the ridge, and the highest peaks of the Karakoram suddenly came into view. After years of reading climbing literature, I recognized the massive mountains along the Chinese border, their flanks heavy and brilliant with snow. The Abruzzi Spur of K2 formed a crisp outline against the sky. It was terrain about which I had dreamed for many years—in my eyes, these were the greatest mountains in the world.

The snow was deep, up to my knees. I kept pushing our track upward toward the highest point.

Finally, the world below fell away, and for an instant, all that existed were these high points of ice and snow and light. At 1:00 p.m., I stood on the summit of K6.

Instead of a metaphor, what stood before me was the real world, the incredible planet on which we exist. As I pulled in the rope, I looked around—in all directions the mountains surrounding us jutted into the heavens as one of the planet's most immense and inspiring forms. I cried at its beauty, and when Scott came up, I grabbed him in a deep embrace. In a life built to seek out peak experiences, this was it—*the zenith.*

We still had many careful steps to go, but they were all downhill now. At sunset, we packed up our tent, took the first of many caffeine tablets, and started rappelling down the west face. There was another rhythm to this stage of the journey, requiring its own clear-minded focus. Sliding into the darkness, I kept my headlamp trained on the ropes, watching for the ends. Again and again, I drilled my anchors deep into the ancient ice and bounce-tested them before committing.

Midmorning, we touched down on the flat glacier. Horsetails of cirrus clouds spun in the sky. The storm was on its way. But for a little while longer, the skies remained clear as we sat perched on a rock, eating the last of our food.

I looked back at K6, its south face rising abruptly from the glacier, its topography still clear in my mind. Changi Tower, beyond the ridgeline, was already a receding memory, lost in a fog of emotions and stories. Gradually, I realized that even the fleeting sense of brightness atop K6 had begun to dim, like a last star vanishing at daybreak. I whispered a silent thank-you to the mountains as I turned my back to them, accepting hazy recollections as my only lasting experience.

9

Stability, or Something Like It

Shannon and I sat on the patio behind one of our favorite haunts in Bend—a food cart turned brick and mortar that specialized in world street food. The sun was setting and our only intention for the evening was to enjoy each other's company.

"Remember when we had to save for a week to go out and eat at a restaurant?" Shannon asked after ordering a second cocktail.

I smiled, thinking about how we would eat before going out in Seattle, then order the cheapest thing on the menu.

"Yeah, things have changed. I think I like this better."

It had been two years since we'd moved to Bend, and we were feeling well established in Central Oregon. Shannon had started a career in digital marketing, applying her background in environmental engineering and teamwork to technology problems. I had joined up with a colleague in the filmmaking space, Jim Aikman, to launch a small production company. My involvement with POW had also increased.

Through their program, I was learning how to use my stories from the mountains to advocate for climate policy. And I found a pathway through which I could better support the communities of the Karakoram in northern Pakistan—working with an organization that focused on building schools, with a particular emphasis on girls' and young women's education.

I was adding many new things to my life and, in many ways, my climbing suffered. Instead of three expeditions per year, I was down to one or two. But after so many years of focus on climbing, it seemed appropriate to spend time working on the other parts of my life. It was the balance that Steve and Kaj had suggested. And it was the balance I wanted.

Through all this development, I remained drawn to the rarefied air of the high hills. This magnetism that I felt from the unknown corners of the high-alpine environments of our world was something primal. It was natural and pure, an instinct that has been passed down through generations beyond the reach of history. It was possibly misguided, as there are no resources in that space beyond stories and hazard, but it was something familiar. With so many new things in my life, spending time in the vertical environment felt known and comfortable. It felt good.

Back in Bend, Shannon and I were living with a fellow alpinist Chris Wright. Like Mark Allen, he had pursued the arduous process of becoming an internationally certified IFMGA Mountain Guide and now his work took him all over the world. With his insatiable curiosity about world culture and food, this constant travel suited him well. He would come home to Bend a few times a year, full of stories about cuisine and mountains.

Professionally, Chris had chosen a very different path from my own. He climbed both for himself and in service of others, working to help others reach the tops of routes and peaks.

He also felt the same attraction toward the unknown corners of the world's great ranges. Independently, we had both refined this need for exploration and discovery down to a salient and actionable set of parameters. We wanted unclimbed walls that were steep and massive with limited overhead hazard.

"What about the Wrangell–St. Elias?" I asked, as I thumbed through books full of mountain photos.

Chris looked up from his computer and replied, "I'd love to check out those mountains."

We were sitting across the table from each other in his home in Bend. The warm Central Oregon light flowed through the windows. Steam rose from our espressos.

"Look at this group," he said, pointing at the screen. "Those look very steep." He zoomed in.

Generally speaking, I had found that the best way to discover new, unclimbed lines was to get on top of a mountain and look around. This method had repeatedly pointed me in the right direction while climbing in the Alaska Range. Our route on Mount Bradley had led me to a series of other routes in the Ruth Gorge, while our time spent in the Lacuna Glacier system had led to a series of incredible objectives. We had been the first to see them, and subsequently we had been the first to climb them.

By this time, I had taken nearly a dozen expeditions into the Alaska Range. I was ready for something new. Hence, Chris and I were looking at images of a range that neither of us had ever visited. The Wrangell–St. Elias, far to the east of the Alaska Range and shrouded in secrets, presented just the potential for adventure that we sought.

"It looks like those peaks are the Twaharpies," I said. "It looks like there's a lot of unclimbed terrain."

A detailed scan of the maps drew us to a peak that we'd never heard mentioned, Celeno. A jagged and severe mountain, Celeno Peak was named after one of the three Harpies of Greek mythology: fearsome beings sometimes described as creatures with the bodies of birds and the heads of women, other times as strong and sudden winds.

Emails and calls with community members revealed that a famous climber of a previous generation, Carlos Buhler, had attempted Celeno's west face, a strikingly steep 6,000-foot wall. We emailed him asking if he would be open to sharing an image. He responded within an hour. The image he shared was severe, but we were able to draw a line up the wall, linking ribs of rock with snow flutings. We made plans to attempt the face.

▲

THE FOLLOWING SPRING Chris and I skied toward Celeno in the near darkness of the Alaskan night. The face loomed above us at the head of the Canyon Creek Glacier, its streaks of dark blue and gray rising to block out the starry sky. Our aim—a subtle spur on the west face—began just above the base and continued nearly to the summit, pointing directly at its apex.

When preparing for the trip, I was impressed by Chris's attention to detail and the variety of systems he brought to the table. It had been a number of years since I'd climbed with mountain guides, but I remembered being impressed by their balance between technical climbing ability and the systems they used to keep themselves safe. It was something I had seen with both Mark Allen and Ian Nicholson: they were not just focused on the size of crimp they were grabbing or the steepness of the ice, but they also loved to geek out on the rope systems they used.

As we prepared, Chris and I had very stimulating and informed discussions about how to handle the ropes, what gear to bring, and how specifically to transition both up and down the mountain. I brought what I learned from my time on search and rescue, climbing with other guides, and nearly 25 expeditions; Chris brought the latest from the American Mountain Guides Association. As we stepped onto the climb, we were well prepared physically and our systems were dialed in.

We climbed the first 2,000 feet of snow and ice unroped. A serac lurked high above us on the face, and for a few hundred feet we had to duck under its hazard. We moved as fast as we could, crossing the area of its potential fall line in less than 15 minutes. By 7:30 a.m. we were roped up and moving into more challenging terrain.

I took on the day's first set of pitches, which wove through blocky rockbands interspersed with winding veins of thin ice. As I hooked my ice axes on small edges, making the final moves out of a steep chimney, I glanced up to see a snow slope leading to the rockband that we'd imagined to be the crux of the route. From this close proximity, I could now see it was very steep and blank.

That night, we slept on a small ledge chopped into a thin rib of snow. Three sides of the small platform dropped away into the void. We slept hard, resting for another big day ahead of us.

In the morning light, Chris led off. One hundred feet higher, the granite of the lower half of the route met the metamorphic rock of the upper half. A dark and severely overhanging headwall shadowed the way ahead.

Chris led two moderate traverses toward what appeared to be a weakness in the rockband. He then headed up onto the headwall.

For the next three hours, he tiptoed over loose rock toward a black roof. Small rocks showered down as he inched upward. With 10 feet of climbing remaining until he reached a large ledge, he hung from a cam, placed into a crack. Pushing upward, he tried to tread as lightly as possible while reaching up to make the next placement, but in doing so, he dislodged a barrage of stones.

I hung onto the rope and cowered at the belay as hundreds of pounds of rock showered down the pitch. Once it abated, I looked up. Most of the rock had fallen 20 feet to my left. Chris was still hanging from the cam, but below him the falling stones had wreaked havoc. One of his ropes was badly damaged, with three feet of bright white core hanging in space. The equipment below had been smashed, including one carabiner that was visibly broken in two.

"Chris! Are you okay?" I yelled.

"Fuck!" he yelled back. "Yes! I am okay . . . but *fuck!*"

Slowly he pulled himself together and I helped him manage the damaged ropes. I then watched in amazement as he finished the pitch. I followed, free climbing and jugging, until I found Chris—shaken, but in one piece—standing on a small shelf above the overhang. I gave him a big hug.

Because we needed to locate a safe place to bivy for the heat of the afternoon, I continued for two more pitches of easier rock climbing to reach what turned out to be our best option—a ledge no larger than two duffel bags set next to each other. We happily slumped onto it and I started melting snow into water to drink. My mind relaxed slightly as I gazed up at the spur, now icy and less than vertical. But the summit was still 2,500 feet above.

It was warm, warmer than we had anticipated, so we decided to keep climbing at night. We left the ledge at 2:00 a.m., and I led through a final two pitches of positive drytooling before the route changed from rock and mixed climbing to steep snow and ice. We simul-climbed to the top of the spur, then cut a hard right to reach an iced gully that led toward the apex of the peak.

At this point, we once again had to duck under the serac that hung over the face. Now it was only a few hundred feet above us. Its ice glistened menacingly. As we sprinted upward, the angle never relented—a steady 70 degrees with short sections breaching into overhanging ice and snow. A light fog began to form, and soon we couldn't see more than 100 feet. All around us towers of rime blocked our way as we continued to simul-climb, following our instincts, toward what we hoped would be an easy exit onto the summit's snow slopes.

When I looked up again, feeling the warmth of the early afternoon creeping into the foggy air, I cursed: a clearing revealed that we'd been climbing into an amphitheater ringed on all sides by overhanging rime. But, as the gap in the mist shifted, I could perceive a ramp to our left. I traversed to it and rejoiced as the terrain slowly started to roll over into low-angle snow. Two hundred feet later, I was standing on a nearly flat ledge. Through the moisture-laden air, I could see the outline of the summit just above me. I belayed Chris up, and he sat down in the snow next to me. Finally, we could relax. With most of the mountain below us, we were, at least for a moment, safe.

Because of our fatigue and the lack of visibility, we bivied on this ledge for the rest of the day and evening. Our forecast had been for clear weather, but the clouds were concerning. The descent from the summit was a complex three-mile ridgeline leading to a very specific couloir that we would need to rappel. If a storm was coming in, we needed to know about it. I pulled out the sat phone and called Shannon.

Her phone rang just twice before she picked up.

"Hey, Shan, we are totally safe and at the top of the wall. But we're in a cloud. Our hope is that it's just some moisture around the summit, but just in case, can you check the weather?"

By this time, our fast-paced, no-fluff satellite phone conversations were well practiced.

"Yup, I'll check," she replied. "Call back in five."

"Great, talk to you in a minute," I said. She hung up and I paused. Something was wrong.

There had been an unfamiliar tone to Shannon's voice. Like she had just been crying.

Five minutes later, I called her back.

"How are we looking?" I asked.

"Weather is clear and the forecast is holding," she said. "It looks like you have a cloud hanging around the summit. It's just some convection or something like that. You should be all set for the descent."

"Great. Thanks, Shannon." Then I paused. "Is everything okay?"

She asked why I was wondering. I told her that I could hear it in her voice.

"Damn it," she said quietly. "I was trying to mask it. Grandad just died. The family is out of town. It's just me here in Portland with Grandmother, trying to manage everything, and I'm devastated."

"Oh man, Shannon, I am so sorry. I'll call when we get to base camp and get home as fast as I can."

"Okay," she replied. "Prioritize safety, Graham. I want you home soon, but I need you home in one piece."

I told her I loved her, and we hung up. I then looked at Chris, sitting next to me on our little snow ledge.

"Wow," I said, "I did not expect that."

"You okay?" he asked.

"I am. Let's stay focused and get off of this mountain safely."

"Deal."

On May 15, we climbed the final few hundred feet to the summit in the predawn light. The clouds had cleared, and mountains spread before us as far as the eye could see. I had managed to focus in on the task at hand. Looking out at the view, I shook my head at our luck and the absurdity of our position.

As far as we knew, there was no one else in the range. We were alone, at the top of a huge wall in a turbulent sea of rock, ice, and snow. It didn't matter that, by this time in my career, I had been in this position many times—each summit proved itself as unique and beautiful as the climb beneath. It was the apex of the experience, the farthest from safety, and besides survival and climbing partnership, it was the ultimate goal. For a moment we allowed ourselves to give in and rejoice as we chanted at the mountains around us.

Twenty-two hours later, we stumbled into base camp. By then, we'd traversed the more than three miles from the summit to the top of the couloir by which the first ascent of the peak had been made. A series of rappels from the ice running down the gully allowed us to reach the glacier below quickly and safely.

The dark form of Celeno loomed above us once more. The streaks of ice and rock were now familiar to our tired bodies and dull picks, but the structure and relief remained terrifying. I was happy to be back down on the ground.

This had been the first time Chris and I had climbed together, besides cragging on single pitches at Smith Rock and our beloved "Crag of Doom," near our home in Central Oregon. On this trip, we had climbed well and we had climbed smart. I expected it was the beginning of a fruitful climbing partnership.

But it was time to get home.

The following morning the weather was still clear; we called the pilot. He flew in off the glacier and dropped us off at a remote airstrip where we'd left our car. We drove straight to Anchorage—eight hours of winding roads plagued by frost heaves in the asphalt.

I called Shannon once we got back into cell phone range. Her parents were trying to get home from England, where they had been on vacation; her uncle would be there soon. In the meantime, it was just Shannon and her grandmother, Carol. They were both sad and overwhelmed by Shannon's grandfather's passing, and in need of support. Despite the remoteness of my current location, I was the closest support available. I pushed the gas pedal down a little harder.

I caught a flight out of Anchorage that night. Chris, being a very considerate friend, took much of the gear back to Bend. I got into Portland late and took a cab to the retirement home where Shannon was staying with Carol.

By the time I slipped in the door, everyone had long since gone to bed. The small living room of the apartment was only faintly lit by the ambient light of the city coming in through the window. I had not stopped moving since finding out about Milt's death three days prior. I lay down on the small, floral-fabric couch and fell sound asleep.

I woke in the morning to find Shannon making coffee in the apartment's kitchenette. She was slowly going through the familiar motions. I got up and gave her a hug. I held her tight and felt her relax into the embrace.

"Hey, darling, how are you doing?"

"I'm okay," she responded. "This is hard."

She offered me a coffee as Carol came out of her room. Normally a happy older woman full of life and stories, Carol now looked to be carrying a heavy weight. She quietly thanked me for making it home so quickly. We all sat down and drank our coffees while watching the day begin through the window.

Having barely slept since summiting Celeno Peak, I felt myself sink into the couch. I had made it home in one piece and Shannon needed my support, but right then I needed a moment to be quiet and be still.

After five minutes, I got up and drank two more cups of coffee while standing at the counter.

"Shannon and Carol, what can I do to help? What do you need?"

Over the next few days, I helped wherever I could—heading out to grab meals and groceries or connecting with Shannon's folks as they made their way back from England. In the midst of loss, I found myself focused on action in a way that was uncomfortably familiar. I also watched Shannon and her grandmother grieve. Their pain was raw. My reaction was different: numb and well practiced.

The list of friends and acquaintances lost in the mountains had grown slowly over the years but had recently been accelerating. Mike had fallen while soloing in the Sierra. Chad had been hit in the face while rappelling down the *Supercouloir* on Fitz Roy. Joe had fallen off a cornice in Nepal. Justin had slipped while descending in Nepal. Scott and Kyle had disappeared in that storm on the Ogre II in Pakistan. I tried to count them on my fingers, but quickly ran out of fingers as I remembered more and more. Some were close to me, others were just acquaintances. All of them had gradually numbed me to loss.

I remembered an essay written by Mark Twight titled "Heaven Never Laughed." In it he discusses dealing with the death of his friend and climbing partner Philippe Mohr: "I tried not to harden myself against it. I studied his accident as thoroughly as the other ones. I dwelled on it because I want to live. Grief is allowed but a small toehold here."

The essay was included in his compilation *Kiss or Kill: Confessions of a Serial Climber*. It came right after another essay, "The Abattoir," in which he describes his own death. I had first read it when I was 18 years old, staring down the barrel of a life dedicated to the mountains. I'd read the book over and over again, and wondered at a life lived so close to the edge that some of us would not survive. It was romantic, it was muscular; I wanted to exist among those brave souls who toed the edge.

Now I sat looking at Shannon and her grandmother. No longer 18 years old—I was 30—I was filled with memories of lost friends, each of whom I had granted only a small toehold of grief.

I knew I was still in love with climbing, but I needed to ensure that I came home in one piece. I scolded myself for decisions that had nearly killed me in the past. I vowed to learn from them, to keep my mind and body sharp. I hoped I was mature and smart enough to survive.

Months before, Shannon and I had made a deal that I would go on a multimonth expedition every other summer. This left the alternate summers for us to spend together, building our relationship and creating our own memories.

She rationalized that it would give me more time to rest and prepare, more time to ensure that my mind was exceptionally well sharpened, ready for the edge. From a strictly operational perspective, it made sense, it was an even balance. I liked the concept.

The following summer, I was planning to head back to the Karakoram with Steve Swenson again. As we started to plan the trip, I was thinking about what it would take to survive. It would require the right partners, the right objective, and the right attitude.

My climb with Chris in Alaska had been a good test run to see if he was the right person to invite on the trip. Steve and I had formed a powerful partnership on Changi Tower, and he wanted to go back. Scott Bennett wasn't available.

Eventually, when Shannon's parents had arrived back in Oregon, we went back to Bend. The drive was quiet. We watched as the landscape transitioned from the lush forests of the western slope into the arid high country of Central Oregon. We were exhausted and ready to get home.

When we finally arrived, I made tea and Shannon settled in for some alone time to recharge.

I went to the backyard and called Steve. I had texted him about the death in the family. He greeted me with compassion, asking how Shannon and her family were holding up. Exhausted from thinking and talking about death, I thanked him and quickly moved on to the reason for my call.

"Chris is smart, strong, kind, and motivated," I told him. "I think he's our guy."

"Alright, great," Steve replied, not missing a beat. "Let's get into planning."

10

The Link

I hung by my harness from a small pedestal of rock as a heavy stream of fine snow poured over me. Icy crystals flowed into gaps between my gloves and cuffs and down the neck of my jacket, chilling my body. I drew my shoulders together. The ropes in my numb hands led upward. Fifty feet away, under the same barrage, Chris clung to his ice tools with his hood up and his head down.

We were 7,000 feet up the 11,000-foot southeast face of Link Sar, an unclimbed 23,000-foot peak in the Karakoram Range of Pakistan, near the contested border with India. Along with Steve, we'd spent two months trying to climb this mountain in a clean and lightweight style, struggling to find a path free of avalanche danger. We had clambered up ridges that wound to nowhere or that ended in slopes under the threat of seracs. Eventually, we found a route relatively safe from overhead hazard. But intense storms pinned us down again and again, far below the summit.

We'd extended our expedition by a week for this final attempt to climb the peak. This was our last chance before the start of autumn blizzards that would engulf the mountains in deep snow. Steve had decided to stay in base camp; he thought Chris and I had a better chance of reaching the top as a team of two. The day before a predicted weather window, we'd started climbing back up from base camp: we'd hoped to summit and descend before storms enveloped the mountain again. Now, as the spindrift slid past my face, I gasped for breath. Chris had been in the same position for 45 minutes, hunched under the ceaseless stream of fine crystals. It was time to end our vigil.

"I don't think the weather is getting better!" I yelled into the maelstrom.

A burst of expletives erupted from above. Chris evidently agreed with my assessment. We were both nearly hypothermic. The decision to bail was an easy one.

When we staggered into base camp, Rasool and Nadeem embraced us. As Rasool smiled, wrinkles spread on his mountain-worn skin. Steve, standing nearby, gave us a knowing look. I knew what he was thinking: by making it down safely, we'd achieved the primary goal of the expedition—to survive.

"Excellent work," Steve proclaimed. "And don't worry, we'll be back."

Two days later, harsh sunlight washed out the gray hues of the rocks and the small patches of green that surrounded our tents. The upper elevations remained another world. High winds spun dark clouds around the summit of Link Sar. The forecasted lull never arrived. Wildflowers wilted in the meadows around us. Winter was approaching. I knew it was time to go home, but the sharp angles of Link Sar still flickered through the mists, as tantalizing as ever.

We'll be back, I thought.

Every climber sees the mountains differently. Some may see a vast collection of peaks, connecting at their edges like waves in an ocean. Others may see only the minutiae, their eyes searing in on a single, ice-laden corner or rib of marbled snow and rock. I had recently come to the realization that I have my own very specific perspective of the mountains. Since I became a climber, many mountains had remained in my mind only as fragments of vast panoramas of glacier-carved uplands and valleys. Occasionally, one peak stood out from the others—a lodestar that lured my imagination on countless dream voyages. Its face appeared like a remnant of some distant, forgotten realm, a shadowy landscape that vanished in the waking world. It was these peaks on which I focused, each a center point for both my memory and my motivation.

▲

I HAD MY initial glimpse of Link Sar in 2015, from high on Changi's north ridge. In the moments between torquing our ice picks into frozen cracks and tapping them into thin ice, we had been able to gaze at the colossal breadth of the central Karakoram, expanding as we gained altitude. Link Sar's summit stood out as a pyramid on the near horizon, sheer and pointy, almost crystal-like in its sharp geometry. Below this sharp point, its southeast wall dropped away. Crisp ridges of ice, rock, and snow radiated downward for over 11,000 feet from the apex into the valley below.

This area had remained closed to foreigners because of the decades-long conflict between India and Pakistan along the Actual Ground Position Line—the approximately 68-mile boundary established in 1984 across the Siachen Glacier region. I wondered if there was a way to gain access. As it turned out, I had not been the only one pondering this question. Steve had seen the same view. In his case, however, the image hadn't left a new impression in his mind. It had invigorated an old one.

Mountaineering teams had applied to climb above the Kaberi Glacier since a 1979 Japanese attempt on the east face of Link Sar. But the Pakistani government didn't offer permits again until 2000, when an American expedition was unexpectedly given permission to travel there. They ended up scaling the southeast wall of a tower at the mouth of the valley, a peak they named Tahir after a particularly helpful local military official. When they returned home, team member Jimmy

Chin told Steve about the giant mountain farther up the valley—the still little-known Link Sar.

A year later, Steve tried to climb the mysterious peak with a team of five other Americans. Well over 3,000 feet below the summit, they reached a dead end—a key couloir turned out to be loaded with hanging ice. They shifted their focus to the rock towers on the opposite side of the glacier, where they climbed long, thin cracks that soared toward a crest of pointy summits, which also proved to be out of reach.

The southeast wall of Link Sar stuck in Steve's mind as a riddle to solve. Near the end of that expedition, he scrambled up a different approach to the wall, through lower bluffs and ibex pastures. Just below the steepest part of the southeast face, he studied the convoluted ridges, hanging ice, and intricate buttresses. The immensity of the problem appealed to his analytical mind and his patience for massive projects. In 2015, he observed the same features again from Changi Tower, and thought he could see a passage to the summit through the steep ribs and dark buttresses that avoided the hazard of the wall's massive hanging ice cliffs. Etched with ice, their convex angles appeared to jut beyond the fall line of the debris. After we'd returned from that trip to Pakistan, Steve sent me a photo of Link Sar. In his opinion, he said, it was "one of the last great unclimbed peaks, particularly in the Karakoram."

To prepare for the expedition, Steve, Chris, and I met up in the Canadian Rockies. As our tools swung into ice and hooked on small limestone edges, we found an easy rhythm. With his decades of experience, Steve tempered our enthusiasm for routes that might have been hazardous. I trusted him, and I assumed his role would be to contribute this kind of expertise, while Chris and I would provide the youthful energy needed to get to the top. To my surprise, when we arrived at the crux pitch of an overhanging frozen waterfall, Steve asked in his calm, mild way, "Mind if I take the lead?"

Chris and I craned our necks. Beyond the shadows of the small cave where we stood, the ice hung rotting in the sun. I could hear the relief in both our voices when we agreed. Steve didn't climb fast, but he also never hesitated. He appeared at home in this steep, fragile world of opaque ice, yet keenly aware of the consequences of underestimating it. With each strike of his axe, he waited patiently for the placements he needed for safe upward progress. This was how we were going to climb Link Sar: one deliberate move at a time, until each crystal and grain of ice, snow, and rock added up to a 23,000-foot mountain.

Of course, we weren't sure we'd ever get permission to attempt the peak. No one had been allowed to access the east side of Link Sar since 2001. All subsequent teams had approached from the west, including two Brits, who attained a subsummit they named Link Sar West in 2015. But after extensive negotiations with the ministry of tourism and the Pakistani Inter-Services Intelligence agency, we managed to procure a permit. By the first week of July 2017, we stood on the Kaberi Glacier, looking up at the same foreshortened view of steep, white snow; angular, dark rock; and hanging blue that Steve had seen 16 years before.

Two months dedicated to the wall were illuminating. Many attempts on the lower bastions of the face were required to find a pathway that was both feasible and safe. Slowly, the mountain had given up its secrets, and by the beginning of August we felt that we were in position to attempt the line. But moisture and storms had rolled into the range, and by the end of the month, we had retreated after reaching only 20,000 feet, making us the ninth expedition to fail on the peak.

I returned to Bend. During the nearly three months I was gone, Shannon had closed on our first house, a single-story dwelling in a small development. Due to my absence, she had finalized the inspections and mortgage documents, signing for me under power of attorney. When I arrived home, we owned a 1,600-square-foot house, empty except for a new mattress. The yard, merely a postage stamp, was bare dirt surrounded by a fence.

On my way back from the expedition, in Islamabad, I had purchased a handmade Persian-style rug. In an attempt at gallantry, I unrolled it in the nearly barren living room. I knew she had been doing heavy lifting on the home front and I wanted to make it up to her.

"It looks great!" Shannon said as she shook her head at me, smiling. She was clearly happy I was home. I also knew she enjoyed a quiet house, which was antithetical to the loud energy I brought. As we went to work finding furniture to fill out the rest of the house, we became reacquainted with each other. It had been a long trip, and now it was time to shift my attention away from expeditions and focus on Shannon and making a home together.

While I was gone for the summer, Shannon had also put down a deposit on a new puppy. I was unsure about having another being in the home at first, particularly one that would be excellent at making messes but never able to clean them up. But when the 10-week-old, cinnamon-haired ball of fluff arrived, my feelings quickly changed. We named her Pebble.

As I was talking to Sam, a friend from my days in Yosemite, he reminded me that I once ended a romantic relationship stating, "You know, man, she's in a different place. Like, she has *furniture*."

"Graham, my friend," he said, "not only do you have furniture, you also have a puppy!"

Shannon and I worked well together as we made decisions about the house. Due to our deal that I would only go on a multimonth expedition every other year, we were looking at nearly two years of time that would be dedicated toward our careers and relationship. During the day, she made deft insights at her marketing job, while I explored new ways to grow my filmmaking business. I learned to design larger-scale projects, pitch them to clients, and execute on the final product.

Occasionally, I pitched stories about my own adventures. Contemplating my relationship with Shannon, I was fascinated by the journey on which we were engaged: two athletes, in different sports, seeking a middle ground, a place where we could grow our partnership and our love. We had found this in *shoshin*, the Zen concept of beginner's mind, an attitude of openness, eagerness, and lack of preconceptions when studying a subject.

Our skill discrepancy was too large for us to ever participate as equals in Frisbee or climbing. If we were going to enjoy outdoor activities together, we needed to find something new. We tried mountain biking. We were awful at it, but we were on the same level and, as we practiced, we improved quickly, and that progression was ours to share.

After a few months of learning to ride mountain bikes, we found ourselves wanting to get away from the manicured trails close to our home in Bend. We wanted to get out into the wild. We had friends who had been going on huge, multiday bike adventures with all their equipment mounted to the bikes. They called it bike packing.

"How do you get into it?" Shannon asked our friend Mason.

"Honestly," he said, "it's pretty simple—you just need to go."

In the spring, Shannon and I drove out to a remote corner of Oregon with our bikes and a new set of frame bags. Neither of us was particularly proficient, having only just started mountain biking a few months before, but we found it a lovely way to cover ground.

By this point in our relationship, we had been on many trips together but never something so close to an expedition. Each of us had experience in the backcountry—mine in the mountains, hers on academic fieldwork jobs in Oregon and Costa Rica—but this was our first time combining our expertise in this way.

"Let's make sure the tents and raingear are on top, in case we have to build camp quickly," I said, leaning into my background full of big storms.

"Sounds great," she said, squinting as she looked out on the rolling hills and steep gulches of eastern Oregon, "I just need to make sure my snacks are easy to get at. Staying on top of my nutrition is a major priority."

Departing on bikes laden with camping equipment felt sluggish. We rode the brakes on the downhill inclines, unsure of our ability to handle heavy bikes, and the hill climbs were a grind. But Mason had been right. We just needed to go, and keep going.

The riding was technical enough to require our full attention as we pedaled across the vast high desert plateaus of blowing sagebrush and through remote valleys of volcanic rock. That first evening, as the lucent, late-afternoon sky began to turn to dusk, we unpacked our bikes and cooked dinner. Sitting on our sleeping bags, time passed quietly as we held hands and gazed out at the lengthening shadows around us. This is it, I thought—this is *love*.

The following morning, we woke to the pattering of rain on the tent. I sat up and made coffee in the tent's vestibule as Shannon peeked out of her sleeping bag.

Neither of us felt like starting the day's ride, but it was Shannon who, once caffeinated, sat up and smirked at me.

"We might as well get going," she said, pulling on her bike shorts.

Away from the constant onslaught of work and responsibility, we found ourselves totally comfortable with each other. As we dealt with fatigue and pushing the bikes through knee-deep mud, the trust that existed between us was obvious and well established.

Far from the scrutiny of society, under a clearing blue sky, in a massive amphitheater of vertical orange stone deep in the wilds of the Owyhee Canyonlands, I picked two pieces of grass and asked Shannon if she had an interest in climbing to the top of a small tower of stone and asking each other questions.

Surrounded by nothing but the wind blowing and millions of acres of wilderness, we asked to marry each other. We tied the blades of grass around each other's ring fingers.

I made a film about the trip, but I left out our marriage proposal. That we kept to ourselves.

I called Nick when I got home. "Dude, Shannon and I just got engaged. I *told* you I knew what I was doing."

He laughed, and kindly did not disagree.

▲

IN THE SPRING, Shannon and I were married in the arid juniper forest to the east of Bend. It was a tiny ceremony, a total of 12 people, including us. Everyone was family, with the exception of Forest, who flew in to take photos, and one of Shannon's former Ultimate teammates, Julia, who drove out to act as officiant.

The family stood in a circle, with Shannon and me in the center. Neither of us had a cultural or religious ceremony that felt meaningful, so we had worked with our families to craft our own. Each person shared a small blessing for our future and a small memento by which to remember that perfect and ephemeral moment in the barren Oregon desert. These were collected in an earthen jar for us to keep as a reminder of the day. We then spoke vows to each other based on those used in Buddhist ceremonies—not because we prescribed to the faith, but because we felt they better represented our relationship, one in which we each stood on equal footing, both providing and needing support in our own unique ways. We said "I do" and smooched in the middle of the circle, before it collapsed in on us in a giant group embrace. We started our marriage immersed in love. It was an auspicious beginning.

Having a year off from expeditions gave me time to reflect on what I valued in climbing and for the rest of my life. I was still climbing constantly, and taking smaller trips to ranges within driving distance, but my mental headspace expanded dramatically. With the additional time, and Shannon's partnership, I was able to start planning in a way that I had not been capable of in the past when I was always on the go. But the dark side of climbing was always close at hand.

▲

HAYDEN KENNEDY AND I had not climbed together in many years, but we continued to stay in touch. He had made some amazing ascents, but more recently his attention seemed to be in Bozeman, Montana, where he had met the love of his life, Inge Perkins. They were carving out a life for themselves, and the stories I heard were of them baking bread in their new home and climbing at local crags. I had not yet met Inge, but it was clear that Hayden thought the world of her.

When I looked at his new focus on home and relationship, I saw a reflection of my own progression in which the mountains remained important but were no longer my sole focus. For me, my partnership with Shannon had proved a powerful counterpoint to the constant pressure climbing induced, a practice that forced me to be tempered and patient when the temptation was so often to always go bigger and harder. I saw the same for Hayden. After so many lost partners, I was delighted to see him taking on a balance that might allow him to survive. Not to mention the joy I felt at seeing a friend fall in love.

In the fall of 2017, after I had come home from Pakistan, I learned that Hayden and Inge had been on a ski tour, attempting the north couloir of Imp Peak in the southern Madison Range, just south of Bozeman. It was early in the season; they had started hiking on dirt but, as expected, found the feature filled with snow. Having put on their skis, they had not ascended far when they triggered an avalanche. According to reports, the slab was not huge—150 feet wide, 300 feet long, and 1 to 2 feet deep—but it released above them. They were overwhelmed. When the snow stopped moving, Hayden found himself buried up to his chest. Inge was nowhere to be seen.

Hayden managed to extract himself and desperately probed the debris. He dug with his avalanche shovel, hoping he could find her. Because it was early in the season and risk was low, they hadn't turned on the avalanche beacons they were carrying, making a rescue nearly impossible.

Hayden searched for Inge among the avalanche debris—which quickly set up like concrete—well beyond the window of time in which she could have survived underneath the snow, but he was unable to find her. Stricken with grief, he gave up and hiked out alone.

He drove to their apartment in Bozeman and wrote a heartbroken and despondent 16-page note that included detailed directions to the spot where he had searched in the slide, marked by his shovel and probe. He then took his own life.

The entire community was absolutely devastated.

When Hayden and I had climbed together, I found myself looking up to him—despite the fact that he was younger than me. Over the years, as he had found his footing in the world's big mountains, my admiration for him had only increased. His ascents, ranging from cracks in the desert Southwest to the soaring peaks of the Karakoram, were groundbreaking. The audacity of his decision to remove an unsightly line of bolts from the upper reaches of Cerro Torre was inspirational. But, of all the exceptional contributions that Hayden brought to our community, I was most deeply affected by his clear-eyed perspective on our shared practice of alpinism.

As he matured, he didn't shy away from talking about his complex feelings about climbing. In the weeks before his death, Hayden had published a short article on the website Evening Sends in which he shared his view on the subject: "Over the last few years, however, as I've watched too many friends go to the mountains only to never return, I've realized something painful. It's not just the memorable summits and crux moves that are fleeting. Friends and climbing partners are fleeting, too. This is the painful reality of our sport, and I'm unsure what to make of it. Climbing is either a beautiful gift or a curse."

It was a statement that I understood, but in many ways, I was not emotionally mature enough to explore it within myself. Instead, after Hayden's and Inge's deaths, I found myself looking at the partners with whom I had climbed and whom I considered part of my generation in the American climbing scene. Some had moved on from attempting hard routes in the mountains, but even more had died while trying to find their limits within them. I was left standing alongside the lonely few who had survived the trials of the practice.

It would have been easy to convince myself that I had made better decisions or that I was a better climber—but I knew that wasn't true. When I compared myself to the likes of Hayden or Kyle, I realized that while decision-making had played a role, so had luck. I tried to define the line between the two, but I could only see a wide swath of gray. It made me worry about my ambitions, but not nearly enough to consider giving up climbing.

Years before, when adopting Kaj's plan, I had never given any thought to the idea of quitting climbing. I would always climb, that much had been obvious. But, as I looked out over the crowd that had gathered to mourn the loss of Hayden and Inge, I wondered if

I had been mistaken. Was the only way to ensure survival to stop climbing?

At the memorial, I talked to Steve Swenson and a few other climbers of his generation. Most of them were finished with climbing the big mountains of the world, having been pulled away by their careers, their families, or their aging bodies.

These guys were the climbing partners of Hayden's dad, Michael. They had all been through the trials of adventure and loss that, I was being forced to realize, were a hallmark of hard alpine climbing.

"Did you ever experience this sense of losing the majority of your generation?" I asked Steve.

"No," he replied. "We all lost partners over the years, but it was nothing like the amount of loss that has been experienced in the American climbing community over the past few years."

They all nodded.

"Is it worth it?" I asked.

They didn't have a clear answer; it was complicated.

While I was sitting with Hayden's mom, Julie, she asked me about Shannon. I told her briefly that all was well, we had bought a house and gotten married. The sadness in her eyes bore into me. She had seen this same future for Hayden and Inge. A future we would never know.

"Julie, I am so sorry," I said, pulling her into a deep embrace.

Years later, having better processed the loss of Hayden and so many others, I wrote a short essay about Hayden that ended with these words:

> *Hayden Kennedy will always be a man whom I will be deeply proud to have known, and a friend I will always be terribly sad to have lost. I will think of his approach when I look at mountain walls and I will think of him when I allow myself to be swept away by love for my wife. He will always be an inspiration for how to cut through the noise of our modern world and define yourself by what is close to your heart. He*

will always be a man I consider to have been the best of us and I will strive to follow in his example.

▲

BACK IN BEND, I engaged with my well-practiced craft of compartmentalizing grief to let it fade while I focused on other things. There was plenty to distract myself with as Shannon and I continued to build a life for ourselves. Both of our careers were booming. She was receiving promotions into leadership positions working as a product manager, and I was working on larger and more complex projects, while also being regularly asked to travel to Washington, DC, to join teams lobbying for climate policy.

I was becoming a spokesperson for the concept of "imperfect advocacy," the idea that we don't need to live carbon-neutral lives in order to be advocates for our climate. Living a carbon-neutral life in the United States is nearly impossible. Instead, we need to decarbonize the *system* in which we live—in particular, the power grid—so we can continue to live fulfilling lives while also being good stewards of the planet. The balance that I was trying to define, between climbing and the rest of my life, was a strong analog to the balance I was promoting between progress and impact.

As part of a team of scientists, policy wonks, and other athletes, I arrived at the offices of our elected representatives with stories of melting glaciers and shorter winter seasons in the big mountains of the world, and of the wildfires in the American West. The goal was to use these stories to grab the attention of congresspersons and their staff, before sharing specifics of how climate change was affecting the health and economy of their districts. Finally, we would ask them to take action, via specific policies.

Some responded with thanks and support, others with skepticism. When we met with alignment, we asked, "How can we help?" The response was almost always to keep working and getting folks to vote. These meetings were oftentimes productive and sometimes enjoyable. During one particularly friendly meeting with a senator in DC, I noticed that he had the *American Alpine Journal* on his sitting room table. I opened it to the feature story about the Changi Tower expedition I'd been on with Steve Swenson; it started with a two-page spread of Rasool's face. That article launched us into a wonderful conversation about the changes we were seeing in the Karakoram. "I am here to work on solutions—not just for me and my climbing, but more importantly for my friends in the Karakoram who don't have the ability to drive change like we do," I explained.

When lawmakers responded with a need for more data on whether climate change is real, or stated that it was an unrealistic priority, we tried to stay calm and find inroads. But sometimes, such as when discussing with my Oregon state representative the links between climate change and the forest fires that were raging across the state, I felt my temper flare.

"Listen," she said, "it is my job to be in the know, and it doesn't feel to me like we have enough evidence supporting climate change or to know if humans are part of the problem."

"With all due respect," I said, trying to stay calm but feeling frustration edge into my tone, "you and I are sitting here with some of the smartest climatologists in the country and they are telling you that it is real. It is. As one of your constituents, I am asking you to do your job to take action to protect us from this change. And on that front, we are here to help."

The conversation devolved from there and, a year later, when we had the opportunity to vote her out of office, we rejoiced at the election of a new, climate-progressive state rep. There were definite wins, along with the frustration.

From DC to Salem, I was getting meetings and having conversations with high-powered officials, wielding my stories to fight for change. Time would only tell if it was working or not, but I was hopeful.

My life outside of expeditions was going well. I was managing to be a reasonable partner to Shannon and a good owner to Pebble, while building a business and operating as a climbing athlete and climate advocate. All the while, I was still becoming a better climber. The list of what I was accomplishing looked like success. But my calendar told me I needed to find more time that was unstructured. Time when I could close my eyes, stretch my body, and take a deep breath.

Looking back over the past 10 years, I could see that most of that unstructured time had been found on expeditions. Times when I was at the whim of the mountains. Times when storms would force me to sit tight, to be quiet and listen to my own thoughts and my body. As I watched my life accelerating, it was clear that I needed a moment to step away. It was time to get back out on a trip. It was a feeling compounded by the vision of the sharp, icy summit of Link Sar and of the path that wound through its elaborate bastions. It was an image that was never far from my mind.

11

Return to the Kondus

Soon after arriving home in 2017, Chris, Steve, and I had begun emailing each other again. There was no question whether we should try to return to Link Sar. It was simply a matter of when and how. As we discussed improvements in strategy, we decided to bring in a fourth partner, Mark Richey.

Like Steve, Mark was in his 60s and had a family. He ran a woodworking business in New England. He'd climbed dozens of new routes in the Andes and made numerous ascents in the Greater Ranges, from ice-laced buttresses in India to snowy faces in Tibet. In 2012, he and Steve received a Piolet d'Or, with Freddie Wilkinson, for the first ascent of 24,642-foot Saser Kangri II in the Indian Karakoram. I didn't know Mark well, but I looked up to him. His addition would help create a balance between the power of youth and the wisdom of age and experience.

Mark's response to our invitation was emphatic: "Let's go do this thing!"

Two months before we departed for the summer, we received tragic news. Three of our friends, three of the best climbers in the world—Jess Roskelley, Hansjörg Auer, and David Lama—had been killed while descending from a new route in the Canadian Rockies. Despite being in the middle of our final training cycle for the trip, Steve and I met up and drove to the memorial in Spokane, Washington.

It was surreal to be there, talking to Jess's mother, Joyce, while on the cusp of a major expedition. I'd first met her at the Piolets d'Or ceremony in France six years before, when Jess's father, John, had been honored with a lifetime achievement award in alpine climbing. We all drank champagne on top of the Aiguille du Midi lift before skiing the Vallée Blanche; it had been an amazing moment. Now we were grieving the loss of her son's life. As I thought about that time in Chamonix, it registered that of the 10 climbers nominated as finalists for the award that year, three were no longer with us. Zdeněk Hrubý had died trying a new route on Gasherbrum I in Pakistan. Ueli had died on Nuptse in Nepal. Hansjörg had died with Jess and David on Howse Peak in Canada. As I talked to Joyce, I didn't mention my upcoming trip.

Outside the reception, I sat with Steve. We were both headed home—Seattle for him, Bend for me—to finish preparing.

"I'm really happy to have you as a partner on this trip," I said.

"Yeah, same to you, Graham," he replied. "Let's not screw this up."

Six weeks later, we were once again on our way to the base of Link Sar, our brightly colored 1980s jeeps jostling up the near-impassable mountain roads maintained by the Pakistani military. As we drove through the lower valleys, we occasionally stopped at schools supported by Iqra, the education nonprofit with which I was working. I was delighted by what I saw: girls in their traditional blue shalwar kameez and white head wraps sitting at desks as their teacher instructed them on mathematics. In one of the classes was Rasool's daughter Fatima, whose school fees my partners and I were paying. It seemed a small act of appreciation for the kindness and care we regularly received from Rasool and his family. In supporting these families, I was following in a long tradition of international climbers supporting local communities.

As we traveled farther into the mountains, Steve peered out the window from the seat behind me, while Rasool hung on to his shoulder.

Outside, the granite wedge of Tahir Tower rose in clean, elegant angles. For a moment, I daydreamed about abandoning our goal and climbing its dry rock instead, with the sun shining on my back.

Farther up the valley, Link Sar was still hidden from view in a dark whorl of clouds. The Karakoram had experienced one of the snowiest winters on record.

When we arrived at base camp, a blanket of white still covered everything 3,000 feet above us. We soon grew accustomed to the din of huge avalanches. I sat in the mess tent with Chris as we tried to read books. "Will it melt?" Chris asked.

"I sure hope so." I stood to gaze out the door at the mountain, its pale flanks dazzling under blasts of solar radiation. *Exactly what we need*, I thought.

The next day after lunch, when we were all in the mess tent, I kept interrupting Steve and Mark to ask questions about the conditions. "Have you ever seen this much snow here?" "What will it take to make it climbable?" "What is the longest you've waited for a mountain like this?" Steve and Mark peered at their books through reading glasses, each immersed in tales of eighteenth- and nineteenth-century history and adventure, but they looked up each time to answer me.

Eventually, I realized how young and impatient I must sound and settled into the more methodical rhythm of a multimonth expedition. My hand stopped reaching for my phone in my pocket. Instead, Chris and I simply listened whenever our older partners talked, and they began sharing more memories of adventures amid the big mountains of the world. Steve described the experience of getting lost with his partners in a storm high on Latok II, only finding their tent by way of dead reckoning down a labyrinth of granite, snow, and ice. Mark recounted how his expedition had made the second ascent of the East

Ridge of Shivling, completing the 56-pitch route a week faster than the first team by bringing less gear and climbing swift and light.

I gradually came to understand that storytelling was a way of imparting indirect lessons. Again and again, the conclusions of their anecdotes reminded me of the core component of alpinism: we are here for the chance to make a dash to the top and back down, but the ultimate form of success is remaining friends and staying alive. It was the same message that Kaj had given me so many years before—abide by the 100-year plan and survive. I felt so lucky to be guided by these mentors.

Yet, as the east face of Link Sar came in and out of view through swirling clouds, I knew there was no way to know what really awaited. At our feet, tarps were laden with hundreds of pounds of the most modern climbing equipment available. Above us, the snow line represented the boundary of a chaotic upper world, where the gold-green light of the meadows faded into dim shadows and pale forms.

Would it be enough?

Our base camp, at 12,000 feet, in one of the deepest valleys of the Karakoram, was dusty and low. The thick air would do little to prepare us for the heights. In our strategy sessions back home, we'd laid out a plan for a well-stocked advanced base camp, about 3,500 feet higher, past a series of bluff-filled meadows where herds of ibex climbed. After a week in base camp, we hired a team of five local porters—Bakir, Jafar, Ibrahim, and two men named Mahmood—to help us carry loads to this site, and we trained them on how to use prusiks on the ropes we fixed through bands of rock.

That season, the elevation of around 15,000 feet put advanced base camp just above the snow line, where the grass soon vanished under six feet of drifts. The porters moved quickly over the path that we'd tramped in the snow; after setting down their loads, they hurried back to the dry valley. On our own again, we excavated trenches and terraces to craft our new home.

Rasool, nearly 70, stayed in base camp. His son Fida Ali and son-in-law Nadeem joined us at advanced base camp to cook and keep us company. During the day, their music blared from tinny speakers as they made tea and played cards. They seemed comfortable in these high hills that I found so intimidating. Their houses were less than 16 miles away, just below the south face of Masherbrum. Many of the buildings in their village were built from the same kinds of granite stones that we now used to construct our tent platforms.

As the fourth week of the 2019 expedition came to an end, they told us about the hard work of looking after their herds of sheep at home and the challenges of living in the Karakoram during the winter, when deep cold and heavy snows settle over the range. They showed pictures on their phones of their growing families, and they laughed and shook their heads when I displayed images of my puppy in return.

Meanwhile, hot sunlight glared off the drifts around us, slowly melting them. In terms of horizontal distance, the summit was only a tantalizing two miles away. The vertical distance included 7,500 feet of some of the steepest and most complex alpine terrain I'd ever considered. While I fretted about the wall that loomed above us, Mark sketched the vast panorama that stretched below: the jagged peaks of Karmanding Brakk and K13 that glinted amid a turbulent sea of rock spires and granite walls. The strokes of his pencil drew accurate contours of the geography that spread before him, but his attention to detail on the steepest buttresses and the highest peaks demonstrated the real focus of his thoughts.

It was July 1 when I heard Mark yell, "Avalanche!" I turned to see a massive, wet slab of snow slide down a bowl 1,600 feet above us. The debris came to a stop well away from our advanced base camp in a jumbled pile of white blocks, some 15 feet high and 1,000 feet wide. Only an hour before, we'd discussed whether it was time to continue up the peak for more acclimatization. Now we paused, frozen in the midst of our tasks, to stare at the billowing snow.

"Guys, I don't think we're going anywhere for a while," Mark said.

No one disagreed.

A week later, glimmers of blue ice and gold-gray rock emerged below the layers of white. Although the probability of large avalanches had lessened, we still needed to adapt before we reached the thin air at 23,000 feet. We saw no easy way to gain altitude along the steep flanks of the glacier. The simplest solution was to start to climb on Link Sar itself. At least there, because of our past attempts, we knew where to go.

We began our acclimatization ascent in the evening, to avoid the heat of the day when the debris of melting ice and dislodged stones fell from above. Chris led through a gash of opaque off-white ice and darker gray rock while the sunset cast hues of orange and purple over the range behind us. Some of our old carabiners still stuck out from the ice from our stormy final attempt in 2017. With a laugh, Chris yelled, "We're redpointing!" and he clipped them to his rope for protection (and subsequent removal).

Once full darkness set in, I led onto the face above, where I found our former passage through icy rock corners and steep snow mushrooms. At times, the familiar route vanished under the drifts. Then I'd recognize a particular seam or edge, and I'd find myself moving in accustomed ways as memories reemerged from two years before. I found a comfortable seclusion in the night. The beam of my headlamp limited my world to the granite and ice in front of my face, and the scratch of my crampons on granite created a familiar rhythm, step after step, as I imagined myself climbing to the beat of the mountain at last. I whooped when I called "Off belay!" to Chris, Mark, and Steve.

We reached our old second camp without mishap, only to discover that what had once been a large, flat ledge of ice had been heaved forward by glacial flow into an incline. A serac hung precariously overhead. As we headed for cover under the swell of a ridge, I noticed how much the thin air had already started to slow us. Our bodies moved sluggishly, as if underwater. Beyond our previous high point, winding crests of snow and ice twisted around steep outcrops of rock and vanished into the unknown. The summit was around 3,000 feet higher, concealed behind a large stony ridge. To my acclimating body standing in the thin air, it felt desperately far away.

Back at advanced base camp two weeks later, clouds poured through the sky in an ever-expanding kaleidoscope of gray hues. Rain came and went. Finally acclimated, we were stuck in camp while storms spilled over the range. The snow continued to melt, leaving a slippery surface of mud and flattened grass around our tents. Even Steve and Mark seemed concerned as they peered out the door of the mess tent into the ashen air. Steve talked about spending 28 days in a storm on K2 in the 1980s, patiently waiting for a weather window that never emerged. Mark told stories of mountains along the Tibetan Plateau that seemed buried under eternal shrouds of snow.

During a lull in the rain, I walked up the hillside with a foam pad and a cup of coffee. My bare feet sank into the soft soil. As I looked across the precipitous sides of the valley above the rock-strewn glacier, I fully focused on the simplicity of the task at hand—to climb this peak with these men and stay alive.

I thought about what it would mean to carry this kind of concentration back to my regular life, as Mark and Steve had been doing for so many years. I looked into my future and thought I saw clarity—a path of exertion and companionship. I believed that spending time in these mountains was about more than just completing a first ascent; these moments would somehow touch my entire existence. Attaining the summit didn't matter. The objective of standing on top of the mountain wouldn't solve climate change or global inequity. In many ways, the risks we took were meaningless. But that seemingly inaccessible point also meant everything to me and to those with me.

The rain started to fall again, and the mountaintops vanished behind smoky clouds. The silvery-gray damp in the air seemed to permeate me with a cold shimmer of doubt. The metaphors I'd constructed in my mind fell apart. What was I really doing here? I rolled up my pad and walked back to camp. I stopped by Steve and Mark's tent and we talked about life at home. I let my mind fill with images of warm, lamplit rooms and the echoes of distant, gentle voices. Steve thumbed his satellite communication device. "Guys, I just got a text," he said. "It looks like we have a window of clear weather on the way."

On July 28, we were back at our second bivouac above advanced base camp. Once again, we scuttled to our tent platforms on an ice rib safe from all but the largest collapse. We moved faster, now; our bodies were more habituated. Still, as the serac barrier reared over our heads, I tried to picture how we would surmount its concave ice in the 20,000-foot air. I winced.

The next day, however, Mark and Chris discovered a less steep path that led around the side of the barrier and onto a tabletop of ice. When it was my turn to lead, I hoped to avoid the overhangs of ice that rose out of a gap between us and the main face like pale monsters in the depths. Finally, I saw a snowbridge that spanned the chasm. I stepped onto the soft surface cautiously. It held my weight.

Once we'd all arrived on the other side, I relaxed into the steady cadence of ice tool placements and crampon kicks into soft ice. Soon, I could feel moisture gathering in the air. Clouds started to close in around us. This time we were prepared; the forecast had warned of another storm, and we'd brought enough food to wait it out. Nonetheless, it felt unnerving to be above 20,000 feet under darkening skies. From the valley, when we'd gazed at the route through a long camera lens, we'd seen a large snowy platform. We hoped it would be safe, although we knew that distant observations and nearby realities aren't always in alignment.

I moved higher and deeper into the swirl of clouds. I first felt the slope start to flatten with my feet, a subtle change in the engagement of my crampons. I surged forward, forgetting that my friends were still simul-climbing on steeper terrain below. I pulled on the rope that connected us, unsure whether I was providing assistance or communicating impatience. Honestly, I didn't care. We'd made it to our ledge, a protruding glacial ice feature, far from any overhead hazard. For the time, at least, we were safe.

In the depths of night, we left that place of security. The forecast called for a clearing. I thought I could sense the grip of the snow and the wind slackening its hold. Instead, the storm tightened its grasp. Six hundred feet above our previous bivy, we sat down in the dark, in a blizzard. The beams of our headlamps reflected off swirling crystals while we waited for a break in the storm or the return of daylight—both seemed far away. Our shoulders slumped forward under the pounding snow.

I could feel our upward momentum grinding to a halt. If we were not careful, such a pause could drag us down the mountain. *Any activity is better than our current inactivity.* I found our shovel and started digging. Steve caught on to my plan, then the others joined in. As I dug, I felt warmer. After an hour, the gusts were still buffeting the mountain, but we were now in a snow cave, sheltered and comfortable, laughing at the absurdity of our situation.

Finally, the sun came up. The morning light sparkled amid a dusting of snow that floated across the air. Shadowy forms of mountains crystallized again. The spindly granite summit of Changi Tower poked through the bright mist; the massive east ridge of Karmanding Brakk crashed through iridescent clouds into the valley below.

Once more, we climbed.

At first, the ice above our snow cave was some of the best I'd experienced in the mountains; with just single swings, my axes stuck. Then the firm surface gave way to fathomless drifts. We clawed upward in the steep, soft snow as our progress slowed and the climbing became increasingly arduous and insecure.

Eight hours later, I stared between my feet—my partners were tied to a feeble anchor composed of a picket buried in loose snow and a screw twisted into soft ice. The rope was strung out for 100 feet between us, attached to nothing. As I dug a path upward, I hoped for a small patch of ice where I could swing my axe or place another screw. Instead, when I shoved in another picket, I tried to suppress the knowledge that if it slid in easily, it wasn't worth a damn.

I looked up to a serac wall that I hoped marked the end of the wallowing; its ancient gray ice undulated in the flat light. It seemed a little closer than it had the last time I'd checked, but still far away. Below my partners, the mountain face plunged nearly 10,000 feet into the depths of the Kaberi valley. To the south, Changi formed a glittering spike of granite and ice against a background of steep walls. I remembered standing on the side of that peak four years before—the security of the ice and stone beneath me, and the wonder I'd felt as I looked over at Link Sar, a fabled unclimbed mountain. What had drawn me to this peak rather than to so many others? Why did it seem so important to stand on a particular point on the vast earth, far away from so much that I love?

Eventually, I reached the security of the serac ice, and a few pitches higher we found a place to bivouac for the evening. It was the early morning, back home. I imagined that the sun was peering over the horizon. Perhaps Shannon was sound asleep, curled up with Pebble.

The following morning, I paused my upward digging. Deep silences lay between my loud gasps in the cold thin air, and in those gaps, I imagined Shannon's and Pebble's gentle breaths. I looked down at my partners. Chris reclined against the snow slope to rest. Mark and Steve hung off the belay and gazed out over the range. They leaned toward the void rather than away from it, at ease in this wild, high realm. I shook my head. It wasn't time to question why I had come to this space. I was here now, and my friends depended on me.

In the early light, the spiry apex of Link Sar turned an eerie blue that seemed to glow just above our bivouac ledge. But as we kept floundering through thigh-deep snow, the summit didn't appear to be getting any closer.

▲

A CRUCIAL PART of mountain climbing is one's relationship with fear. While attempting a first ascent on a high peak, fear is always close at hand, stoked by the exposure beneath your feet, a wisp of wind carrying a cloud across the summit, or the constant challenge of reading the climbing above. *Is that a storm building? Will I be able to find an anchor? Is this pitch possible? Is this pitch too dangerous? Where do I draw that line?*

For experienced climbers, fear becomes a tool. Sometimes the emotion can be dismissed as irrational, but it can also be an alert to subconscious recognition of hazard that might have otherwise gone unnoticed. It can drift into one's mind as a tingle on the nape of the neck or come as a jolt, brought on by a sudden realization or event. It must then be analyzed. *Can I justify this fear through rational decision-making or must I pay heed?* On a big climb, this analysis presents itself over and over again, requiring acute efficiency lest the climber fall into paralysis.

Climbing steep, soft snow is undeniably dangerous and subsequently stokes fear. As I climbed, every modicum of progress was made by reaching my ice tool over my head and jamming its shaft down into the snow, trying to elicit any sense of purchase from the lightly structured frozen water. Digging deeper into the snowpack would sometimes yield better snow, but oftentimes it was just more effort for little gain. Similarly, the footholds were each carved from this same soft, constantly collapsing matrix.

On my lead blocks, I would carefully balance the pressure of my body against the snow as I climbed three feet at a time for pitch after 230-foot pitch. The constant terror of the rope dancing below, attached to nothing between me and the belay, became a numb pounding—I could ignore it, unless something changed.

As I climbed, the surface hardened, abruptly, while I was leading. The purchase in the snow felt more secure and I quickened my pace. Moments later, I felt a sudden confusion—the snow in front of me was shifting, its grains trickling like sand. For an instant, I thought I was hallucinating due to the altitude. I then realized I was standing on a slab that had been hidden amid the mountain's wind-blasted undulations. Now, it had broken off and begun to slide.

There is a rule in mountain climbing: the leader cannot fall. Unlike rock climbing at the local cliff, the risks of falling in the mountains are unacceptable—you are oftentimes risking huge falls by making moves far above your gear while covered in sharp tools. To fall is to greatly endanger not only yourself but also your partners, who will have to execute a rescue as they attempt to save your life from nearly inevitable injuries.

I had experienced accidents while climbing, but I had never before taken a leader fall while climbing in the mountains.

As the snow poured over me, I tried to hang on to the mountain, but the stream of debris knocked my axes out of their hasty, shallow placements. "Falling!" I screamed. My partners, around a corner, couldn't see me as I tumbled backward, slid headfirst for 65 feet, shot over a cliff, and free-fell for another 50 feet until the ropes caught over a rib of snow and ice. I stopped in midair, upside down, staring into 10,000 feet of void.

A sense of cosmic solitude filled me as if I'd plummeted into space. My life did not flash before my eyes, I did not think of my loved ones. My mind developed a singular focus on any action I could take that would promote survival. As I was falling, my options had been limited, but when I stopped, I was able to regain some control of the situation. There was no time for fear or worry; that would come later. In that moment, there was only the will to live.

My friends were still invisible, somewhere above. When I yelled toward the belay, I couldn't hear a reply. I righted myself and swung toward the wall to place a cam. If I could unweight the rope, they would at least know that I was conscious. I probed my body, expecting to find an injury, but I only noticed a single missing zipper pull, ripped from a pants pocket. I reached inside—my lip balm was still there. I transferred it to another pocket. That simple act was my first moment of control after the fall.

Eventually, with many shouts back and forth, my partners and I established that no one had been hurt by the avalanche. Two hours later, I was back at the belay in tears. I embraced Steve, Mark, and Chris one at a time. They examined my torso and legs, looking for some injury that I hadn't noticed.

"Man, we didn't know what had happened to you over there," Steve said. He placed his hand on my shoulder. "We're getting ready to go down."

He appeared serene, as though the thought of retreat didn't bother him. Mark and Chris remained silent. From time to time, they turned to glance at the summit, less than 500 feet above. Its remaining ice fields looked insignificant compared to the massive face that now plummeted beneath us. Its apex still gleamed like a blue-white star. I could feel their longing, as well as my own.

"Guys, I'm coming down from a pretty intense adrenaline rush," I said. A chill had crept into my body and my head felt light. "But I'm not hurt. I'm going to huddle into my down jacket and sit on the anchor. If one of you is up for leading, let's go up, because Lord knows there's no fucking way I'm coming back up here after this."

After a short discussion, in which I didn't take part, Chris took over the lead. Avoiding the now obvious portion of unstable snow, he moved slowly and deliberately, trying not to waste any energy. I could tell that he was fatigued from days of exertion at altitude, but a singleminded drive for the summit kept him heading upward.

For the past two months, my mental vector had been clearly defined. I'd had two goals: to make good decisions and to reach the top of Link Sar. Now I felt lost. The majority of the ascent was behind me, but I was scared. The path upward seemed as nebulous as my purpose in following it. I longed for the kind of safety that only existed far below, days of rappelling away. I rarely hand off my decision-making to others, even when the stakes are low. But there I was, high in the Karakoram, placing the responsibility of my well-being completely in my partners' actions. And I was planning to continue even higher with them, despite having just taken a huge fall at nearly 23,000 feet on a giant, unclimbed peak. I was in the hands of my most trusted friends.

Around us, the shadows of the Karakoram mountains lengthened. The air shone with a late-afternoon gold. The rope came tight on my waist. I was on belay again. One by one, I pictured my partners' faces: sunburned, windburned skin; frost-plastered hair; bright eyes. High on the mountain, the differences between our ages had blurred. We each appeared aged by effort and altitude, we were each rejuvenated by friendship and hope. Our separate experiences had merged into one well of knowledge. I trusted these men.

Everything else in my life seemed to have fallen away. I no longer thought of my role as a husband or of the future ahead. I didn't care about the changing climate or its impact. I was rubbed down to my raw essence; my soul was exposed. For those few moments, falling from the mountain, my survival weighed in the balance, but now my vector forward stabilized and my body remained strong. I was scared, but logic told me that I was making a good decision. Deep down, I still wanted to climb Link Sar. I quieted my thoughts, and I headed uphill.

Yet, with each step, I was now haunted by a deep, instinctual craving for security, for myself and for my friends. Three pitches later, when I arrived at Chris's anchor, the bollard around a thin snow mushroom and the picket in soft snow didn't seem like enough to me, compared to the enormity of the mountain beneath our feet. I crawled into a hole in the snow so I could act as a "deadman," a part of the anchor.

The summit was now just 65 feet above us. But as Chris started plunging the shafts of his ice tools into the steep slope, they sheared through loose drifts without catching on anything or creating any tangible pathway for upward progress. He came back to the belay unsure of what to do.

"Is it simply a large cornice?" Mark asked.

"Are we on top?" Steve asked.

Are we failing? I wondered silently.

Mark craned his neck to study the snow that led toward the top. He had experience with this kind of terrain in the Peruvian Andes.

"Mark, I think you're the only one who knows how to deal with this," I said.

"Yeah, I'll go see what it looks like."

Up to this point, I realized, Mark had been holding back his eagerness to lead, knowing that Chris and I could go faster than he could, simply by virtue of our youth. Now his desire shone unconcealed in his eyes—the glint of a much younger man.

As Mark headed out, he seemed to be casting off into a sea of floating, vertical snow. I told Steve that we needed a new anchor for the descent; they were definitely not allowed to leave me as one on the mountain. He smiled wryly and dug deeper into the snow. Nearly an hour later, Mark shouted that he'd reached the summit. Just then, Steve called out that he'd found a deep vein of ice for a V-thread anchor. Our path to the top was clear, as was the first step back toward the safety of advanced base camp. Thirty minutes later, we were all on the apex of Link Sar.

I arrived last, to a deep embrace from Chris. I don't remember sharing much in the way of spoken sentiments or congratulations. We simply screamed to the mountains around us. Sunset cast waves of purple hues over the immensity of the Karakoram. Some of the steepest and wildest mountains of the world unfolded before us in all directions. For a moment, I let myself feel a sense of accomplishment. Maybe we had made the right choice to keep going up after the fall; but I also knew I could never be certain how much of that result was due to luck. No matter how careful and prepared we try to be, luck is always the wild card.

Here and there, rays of dusk illuminated thin crests of ridges: first gold, then pink and violet. Clouds drifted over deep voids. Ripples of light and shadow, snow and stone extended to every vanishing point until the earth blurred with the sky, and in the vastness of it all, I glimpsed the Other, something more essential than success. There were no words, only the afterglow that comes from delving into the depths of shared exertion, inexpressible partnership, and a brush with the end.

Then I declared, "Let's get the fuck off this mountain safely." We started our descent.

▲

THREE DAYS LATER, I sat in the meadow at advanced base camp. Wildflowers exploded around me. After so much time in a sharp-edged, nearly monochromatic world of rock, ice, and snow, I was over-whelmed by the colors and fragrance. Chris, Mark, and Steve sat beside me. We were finally in a place where we could truly rest.

Nadeem and Fida Ali joined us. They'd prepared a celebratory meal of french fries, fried chicken, tuna salad, and chapatis, and they now asked us questions: "Are you okay?" "Do you feel good?" "How was the summit?" They, too, were able to relax for the first time since our departure, nine days earlier. Their relieved smiles belied just how tense their own vigil had been. I pulled each of them into a big hug and thanked them for being there with us.

Steve, Mark, Chris, and I peeled off our shirts in the hot, sunny air. My partners' muscles were worn thin by days of hunger. Their faces were still slightly puffy from the exertion at altitude, but their eyes were sharp from the experiences we'd shared in the heights. In that particular space of exertion and concentration, they'd come to know me better than anyone else ever had. And in that moment, I trusted them with my life. I will always love these men.

Leaning back into the grass, I shut my eyes. I allowed myself to engage with all the emotions I'd kept closed off while I was deep in the focus of climbing. The shelter of advanced base camp felt sweeter than ever. I luxuriated in the softness and scents of the earth around me, the warmth of the sun's rays on my face, the steady murmur of my friends' conversations.

I let my world once again expand to encompass the rest of my life—the joyful flash of Shannon's blue eyes, the waving flag of Peb-ble's tail, the green smell of the ponderosa forests near my home. I understood that the fall I'd taken might forever change my perspective on the mountains. I could no longer think of my exposure to acute risk as merely theoretical; the physical reality of the hazards was now ingrained in my memory.

I stepped away from the group and called Shannon on the sat phone to let her know that we were down safe. It was the middle of the night in Oregon. From her groggy voice, I could tell that I'd woken her from a deep slumber. "Good job, honey," she said. Her tone quickened with delight as she realized we were finally down safe. "I am going to sleep much better now."

I told her I would call again at a more reasonable hour. I stood still for a while, holding the phone.

Even after it went silent, I imagined I could hear the echo of her voice. It was as if I'd taken my first step home. Uphill from me, my partners were texting and calling their loved ones. The news of our success was reaching the rest of the world, and with it we were being pulled away from the experience. Our partnership, which only hours ago seemed like a sharply defined world of its own, was transforming into something more diluted and complex.

I thought back to that certainty I'd felt in this same place, just a few weeks prior, when I imagined a clear path into the future. Now I knew the terrain intimately, but all I recalled was long, murky labyrinths of granite and ice, seracs and chasms. Perhaps such moments of stumbling through uncertainties might be more relevant to actual life in the lower regions than the brief, seeming clarity of a summit view. These were stories of complication and effort that I could use while talking about climate change or encouraging young climbers. In the moment, though, I could still grasp that vision of fleeting beauty, formed of fading light and violet air. I had watched as it vanished, leaving only an afterglow that was growing increasingly dim.

For now, the impression of wonder drifted down the mountain, suffusing the vivid greens of the meadows, the glossy textures of petals and blades of grass. The expansive love that I felt—for my friends, for Shannon, for everything that surrounded me—all this should have been enough joy to sustain a full existence. But I knew well that there was no way to remain in this state of mind forever. My awareness of the reality of risk would soon push me to stay closer to home, away from these mountains. But, as the euphoria of survival dimmed, would I end up convincing myself that I could simply use that experience to make better decisions?

I looked at Steve and Mark, two men who had managed to not only survive but thrive. They had their own versions of the 100-year plan.

Their objectives changed over time, but they always kept their blade sharp so they could hone a fine line between climbing and the rest of life. They loved the mountains while respecting them for the hazards they presented. Their example stood as a testament to the power of balance and survival.

In front of me I saw my own path, following in their footsteps. I had a continuing love for the mountains and a continuing respect for all the lessons they brought to my life, both good and bad. We would never forget those climbers we had lost, and we would continue to learn and climb, as safely as possible, to honor their memories.

And amid the blur of exhaustion and trepidation, I saw another mountain that stood out from the vast panorama I'd glimpsed from high on Link Sar. It rose alone in my mind—attractive, terrifying, and unknown, its ridges of ice and rock struck downward into a deep valley, unseen, far below.

I suspected that my partners, lying in the grass nearby, had also noticed its mass, and that its image was swimming in their fatigue-ridden consciousness as well. I pushed the thought aside. This wasn't the time to discuss new objectives or to engage with the future. It was time to get home, to swing to the far side of the pendulum where things were safe and comfortable.

But I also knew that the mark this next mysterious peak had left on my mind wouldn't disappear. It would only grow and develop until I'd gone to see it close-up—the ridges of ice and rock that soared to a small, pointy summit, and the potential path that wound through the steep ribs and ice-etched buttresses of dark stone.

12

Kichatna

It had been five years since I told Kaj that I wanted to try the West Ridge of K2. We had been sitting in Seattle at his office, drinking coffee and nibbling strong, dark chocolate, when he asked me if I had any long-term goals with my alpine climbing.

"I do have a plan formulating," I told him, "but I haven't told anyone yet."

Some climbers talk about a singular, crystallized goal in their climbing, a particular peak or a certain grade of difficulty. I had never set those sorts of goals, besides improving and surviving, but recently I had been thinking about what I needed to perform to my highest ability. Looking back at my career, I recognized that I liked being at altitude and I didn't mind being patient with big objectives. As a climber I had the ability to move moderately fast on technical terrain. The questions were, How could I combine these building blocks to their highest potential? How could I lean into my strengths to achieve the hardest thing of which I was capable?

Kaj was the perfect person to run my ideas by. He was invested both in my success as a climber and in me leading a long and fruitful life. This was the man with the 100-year plan. He knew the balance; he lived it.

"I think that trying an alpine-style route on one of the world's highest peaks would be really cool," I told him.

"Wow," he said, slowly, "that's huge." He was choosing his words carefully.

"I just don't know if I have the maturity needed to turn around if the conditions are not right when we are high on the mountain," I replied. "It would be very hard. The magnetism of a summit like that will be strong."

There are 14 peaks over the height of 8,000 meters (26,250 feet) on the planet. They reach into what inflammatory made-for-TV documentaries call "the death zone"—the altitude above which almost no life can be sustained. It is the thinnest air that can be experienced while standing on terra firma. All these mountains are located in the high ranges of Asia and were first summited many decades ago, the first being Annapurna, in 1950, and the last, Shisha Pangma, in 1964. The highest two, Everest and K2, were climbed in 1953 and 1954, respectively. But there remained some new routes to be established, and many routes had only been completed in a classic siege style, with thousands of feet of fixed rope and camps stocked by local porters.

I had done a careful audit of each peak, looking for objectives that suited my strengths and fit within my parameters of being sufficiently safe. As I explored the options, I consistently came back to the West Ridge of K2, with its dramatic angle and relatively low objective hazard. It had neither been climbed in alpine style nor been taken to its logical conclusion—directly up the ridgeline to the summit.

I was familiar with the eccentricities of the Karakoram Range in which 28,251-foot K2 stood. I had seen it in person on a few occasions. Most of these viewings were fleeting—as clouds moved in while standing on the summit of K6 West and as the sun set on the top of Link Sar.

It stood as a hulking mass on the horizon, a beacon. In 2019, I had the chance to sit back with it and watch as the day passed.

Having finished our ascent of Link Sar, Steve and I had hiked into a valley above the town of Hushe, looking for future objectives. The peaks above town had not ended up being to our liking, but from a high ridgeline we had caught a stunning view of the upper flanks of K2, or Chogori, as we'd decided to refer to it.

Its mass was unmistakable. The first ascent route on the Abruzzi Spur, came crashing down at a stark angle to the right, and the craggy towers of the *Magic Line*, climbed by a Polish team in 1986, looked impossibly steep as it poured off the mountain in our direction. The left-hand skyline was defined by the West Ridge as it plummeted straight from the summit into the peaks below.

The route looked safe and it looked enticing. This was confirmed by numerous articles and interviews. And as I researched other peaks, I was never able to pull my mind away from the soaring architecture of the ridge. The West Ridge stood supreme in my mind as the climb I wanted to try.

After receiving (in an anticlimactic early pandemic ceremony) that highest honor in alpine climbing, the Piolet d'Or, for our ascent of Link Sar, I felt ready to test the furthest limits of my abilities as an alpinist. I wanted to share my thinking with Kaj once more so I called him. He listened intently as I explained why I felt the time was now right for K2.

"My sense is that this is the next logical step in my progression as an alpinist," I said. "It feels like the right objective and it feels good. I think I'm ready."

So it was that in 2021, at the age of 35, and as the first major wave of the global COVID-19 pandemic eased, I headed to K2 with Ian Welsted to attempt its West Ridge in alpine style. Our ascent went as per plan until we reached 23,000 feet to find astronomically high temperatures. We stopped on a ledge and watched the mountain melting around us. We were under clear azure skies that beckoned us toward the summit, but it was obvious that to climb higher would be an unacceptable level of risk. Disappointed and frustrated, we tore ourselves from our upward trajectory. Despite a painful feeling of deflation, I was glad to have avoided a close brush with our final exit; we heeded the 100-year plan and headed down.

Once safely back in base camp we learned of the many climbers on the standard routes of both K2 and Broad Peak who had not heeded the warm conditions. Some of them had perished due to errors in judgment, while others told tales of near misses. More tragic still was the catastrophe taking place in the foothills of the high mountains as dozens of Pakistani citizens were killed by climate-change–related flooding. We departed base camp, not having gained the summit but grateful to simply be returning with our lives.

After the trip, I sold my stake in the film company and took on a full-time staff role with Protect Our Winters, focusing my work on climate policy. The position was tasked with empowering other athletes to use their platforms as a tool to drive climate policy and civic engagement. Additionally, I became board president for the American Alpine Club. It was a position from which I could encourage other climbers while driving increased social equity within the community. I appreciated the opportunities to focus significantly more of my energy on climate and equity work, aligning my efforts with my values. It also meant less travel, gave me more time with Shannon, and provided a stable schedule from which I could more easily plan training. At the same time, I started using the story of oppressive heat on the West Face as a tool to talk to politicians and my community about the need for action. I found that it resonated.

In these conversations and presentations, someone would inevitably ask, "When are you heading back?" I'd avoid answering, saying my work and marriage were my current focus.

Back with Kaj, a few months after retreating on K2, I was able to be more honest.

"I loved so much about it," I told him. "The peaks were truly the most magnificent geography I have ever seen—the ragged silhouettes of the Karakoram go on forever. And moving quickly over such massive terrain offered this incredible sense of exposure; I felt so powerful yet so insignificant. It felt like what I was born to do in the mountains. But there was so much out of my control. I want to go back, but I'm confident that if I continue to pursue routes like the West Ridge, I'm unlikely to survive."

He nodded, looking me right in the eyes, but didn't respond straightaway.

"I'm not sure what to tell you, Graham," he said eventually, "other than that I'm one of many who are invested in your survival. The work you're doing outside of climbing, your partnership with Shannon, those are the things that need to be weighed heavily against the risks you take."

He paused, looking out the window.

"There are many ways to get at climbing, many ways to push yourself. New routes in the Karakoram are not the only way. Find the path that allows you to balance alpinism with everything else you've invested in. This is your equation to solve, but I don't think you'll ever find the answer. It will always be changing; that's how life works."

▲

AFTER THE EXPEDITION, Shannon and I went to the Oregon coast to spend some time together. We needed time to reconnect.

In the morning I woke up and made coffee. Shannon was still sound asleep, with Pebble now curled up on my recently vacated pillow. I quietly put a coffee next to the bed with a note: "Headed down to the water, back soon. I love you."

The Oregon coast is not an expanse of white sands. Much of it is hard coastline, where storms bash against bastions of rock as they roll off the Pacific Ocean. Beaches do exist, sections of coastline where these storms have deposited sand between rocky headlands, but they are places you're more likely to see Gore-Tex than swimsuits.

Jogging down the beach, I felt springy in my thick neoprene wetsuit. I looked out over the breakers. The waves were disorganized and frothy, full of rotten water. I ran through the skim left from a retreating wave and dove in.

Growing up in the Pacific Northwest, I had never been far from the beach, but the magnetism of the mountains had always pulled in the opposite direction. Later, during university, I started surfing but never became proficient, spending more time getting slammed against the ocean bottom than gracefully sliding down the face of a wave. But there had been moments, mostly out beyond the breakers, oftentimes at sunrise, where I found peace.

As I dove into the cold waters on the Oregon coast and felt the jolt of 50-degree water wash over my face, that peace was where I was headed.

Diving under waves is much easier without a surfboard. I quickly made my way into the peaks and valleys of unbroken waves. There I stopped.

I lay on my back, buoyant in my wetsuit. Staring at the sky of the early morning, I took deep breaths and focused my mind on the smooth, rolling motions of the water and the massive expanse of the sky above me. I closed my eyes and let my body relax. I watched my mind drift, undulating between subjects while considering how I was to move forward. I let myself bathe in the possibilities of the future and release any sort of overanalysis or fear of change.

What is it that you want? What is it that you need?

Back home in Bend a few days later, I drew a line through the progression of my climbing, from the initial climbs in the Cascades of the Pacific Northwest and New Zealand's Southern Alps, through to the heights of the Karakoram. For many years I had seen this line as a clear path along which I gathered the skills and strength to attempt the most severe peaks on the planet, like it was something predestined. As I looked at it now, the route seemed more like a series of choices based on opportunity and inspiration, and the cultural pressure to do better, climb harder, move faster. There were other paths I could have followed, other areas in which I could have invested.

Reading through my journals from my first major expeditions, I was astounded by how young my voice sounded—in particular on my first expedition to Alaska in 2008 with Ian Nicholson and Ryan O'Connell.

We're in fucking Alaska! My goodness gracious!

My inexperience was obvious and studded with expletives.

This place is really big and really fucking full on. Estimating that the face was around 1,800 ft. tall we went light . . . back on the ground we looked up to find our high point and realized that the face was more like 3,000 ft. tall. The "Alaska Factor" was in full effect. Holy shit.

We had spent two weeks on the Cul-de-sac Glacier, nestled into the Kichatna Spires. They were a small clutch of exceptionally steep peaks 70 miles west of Denali along the undulating spine of the Alaska Range. It was an area full of climbing lore.

For many years, the area had been an afterthought, relative to the higher peaks in the range. Eventually, as climbers started to focus on technical climbing rather than the highest peaks, they started to wonder about the ragged ridgeline visible to the west as they flew in to attempt Denali.

In his 1967 *American Alpine Journal* report on the spires, famed alpinist and author David Roberts stated, after making the second expedition to the area, that "no other area combines heavy glaciation, remoteness, and bad weather with such an abundance of vertical walls, pinnacles, and obelisks." It was during this 1966 expedition that two of his teammates made the first ascent of an 8,985-foot peak, the highest in the range, via its East Ridge. They named the mountain Kichatna Spire, after the river that flowed south from that part of the range. Subsequently, the group of peaks around this high point had become known by the same name.

The spire is a jagged and severe peak with huge granite walls rising from the glaciers around it. Its flanks are more reminiscent of the towering walls of Yosemite Valley than most other parts of the Alaska Range. It became a peak that attracted hell-bent individuals who valued technical difficulties over the glory of the world's highest peaks. The subsequent first ascents on the peak represented some of the most technically demanding climbs in the Alaska Range, and only one of these had successfully ascended the peak's dramatic northwest face—the *Ship's Prow*. This ascent of an overhanging blade in the sky by Andrew Embick and Jim Bridwell in 1979 was on the leading edge of applying Yosemite big-wall tactics to the big mountains.

The northwest wall of Kichatna, striking vertically for thousands of feet off the Cul-de-sac Glacier, had been the goal of my 2008 expedition with Ian and Ryan. We had hoped that the snow and ice gully on the far right side of the wall would provide a pathway to the summit. But at its apex, after 1,700 feet of steep ice climbing, we had found ourselves below blank granite covered in rime ice with a storm blowing in through the col.

I had stood there at that col, gripping my ice tools, facing into the gusts of the oncoming storm and staring at the wall above. *If only the weather was good.* But I knew I would have been outmatched, even in perfect conditions.

After an attempt on another peak, Riesenstein, we were caught in storms until the end of our trip. As our departure day neared, the tone of my journals changed from amazement to stress.

Spent the day trying to get picked up, no love except the occasional bit of clear skies. Now it's white out, blowing hard and snowin' hard. F-U-C-K.

Between the journal entries were stark line drawings of the faces surrounding us. White couloirs were edged by aggressive black line strokes from my pen, denoting the walls. They were places of darkness and mystery—I knew neither how to climb on their flanks nor what it would feel like to hang from their incipient features.

In my journals, I brooded over my inspiration. I wasn't unhappy for the storms that crushed our camp, as in many ways they were a welcome excuse not to climb. They were a reason to stay within the confines of our tents, little dots of color on the expanse of the gently flowing glacier.

Eventually, we were picked up and made the quick transition from the land of ice, rock, and snow that dominated base camp to the green grass and flowing water of Talkeetna. We ate pizza and drank whiskey by the river outside of town. I relished our release from the looming towers and massive storms.

With this release, my journals changed tone. Alongside the still shrouded line drawings of the peaks, I wrote notes to my future self:

The Alaska Range left a strong impression on me. While in the Kichatnas, we didn't get to the top of anything, despite climbing almost 4,000 feet of new terrain—wild. If I am going to be successful on walls like these, whether in the Alaska Range or Patagonia or the Karakoram, I am going to need to step up to the plate and get better and stronger. I think I can do it. I am super stoked to get into it. Also, don't bring a book that has anything to do with climbing!

Youthful exuberance and profanity aside, I was, in many ways, correct. In the intervening years, I had trained and I had progressed. That work proved a launching pad for opening new routes. I had tackled huge mixed routes in little-known corners of the Alaska Range, climbed new walls in Patagonia, and summited untrodden towers in the Karakoram, but I had never gone back to Kichatna Spire's northwestern wall.

At home, I sat one evening, reviewing these journals, as Shannon puttered in the kitchen and the dog slept on the couch. I poured myself a glass of wine and pulled up images of that northwest wall. I laughed at my audacity, thinking I could climb such a thing at that young age, before I had seen, let alone climbed, the walls of Yosemite.

In one image, my eye drifted to the buttresses of rock that protruded, then I traced the line we had attempted. The ice-filled couloir had been, at that time, the only thing I could conceive of climbing on the face, and hence I had been happy to bury myself in its depths, feeling safe. But now, looking at the face, I saw the couloirs as the areas of the highest hazard. They were where any falling materials from high on the mountain would collect and therefore were the last places I wanted to spend time.

I instead found myself drawn to the obvious blade in the sky that Bridwell and Embick had climbed and the hulking buttress to its left. Having developed as a climber, I now saw features and recognized what they were—more challenging but also lacking the dangers associated with snow while being rife with the technical trials of steep granite. I zoomed in until the image was badly pixelated. There were features and cracks connected by blank areas. I knew from experience that these areas were unlikely to be totally blank. As I got closer to them, they would reveal smaller features and smaller cracks—but how small and how friable? Would they be climbable?

"Amigo, what are you doing this spring?" I asked Dave Allfrey over the phone.

"Working, being a dad, and trying to get out climbing," he replied. "Whatcha got in mind?"

Dave and I had been friends for more than a decade, both of us having spent time together on the Yosemite Search and Rescue team in the late aughts. He was a long-haired child of Californian granite and sunshine, with a wry wit and a fast smile. And his climbing was incredible. His apprenticeship learning to climb big walls like El Capitan had paralleled my own in alpine climbing. While I had been chasing down mixed pitches in the wilds of Alaska and the Karakoram, he had climbed some of the hardest routes in Yosemite, stood on top of Trango Tower in Pakistan, and opened new routes on the unthinkably large walls of Baffin Island, in Nunavut, Canada.

For years, we had talked about going on a trip together that would combine our specialties of mixed climbing and big walling. While drinking champagne and celebrating the marriage of friends, we talked about going fast on new lines in the Karakoram. At the memorials of lost partners, we drank whiskey and talked about how we should go on a trip and "keep it tight"—no mistakes. During this time, he and his wife Carmen had a baby boy, Dean, whom he was holding as we chatted on the phone.

As we talked, we pored over the image of Kichatna.

"Can we do it in two weeks?" he asked. "And can we maintain wide margins of safety?"

I told him I thought we could.

We decided to invite a third climbing partner, to add even another layer of skill and increase our margins. Our friend Whit Magro was an obvious choice. A few years older than Dave and me, Whit was a broad-set former wrestler who climbed with immense power. Having grown up in Ohio, he had moved to Montana for college, discovered climbing, and never looked back. Now a high-end blacksmith in Bozeman, he spent his free time developing some of the area's most difficult climbs on both ice and rock. He and his wife Kimberly had two children.

"Amazingly, fellas, I have the time, the objective looks good, and I trust you two," Whit said over the phone. "I just need to know that if things get hairy, we're going down."

"Getting home safe and sound is the number one priority," I assured him.

"We've all achieved plenty in the mountains," said Dave. "We've just got to keep surviving."

"Hell yeah," Whit replied. "None of this fast and light, alpine-style garbage. We're going *Daddy style*."

They assured me that, while I didn't have kids, I could still participate.

"Pebble the Labradoodle can act as your stand-in," Dave said, laughing.

▲

SO IT WAS that Dave, Whit, and I, along with a young photographer named Oliver Rye, flew onto the Cul-de-sac Glacier on May 23, 2022.

Our trip to the small town of Talkeetna had been filled with easy banter about family and dear friends, both with us and lost.

In Talkeetna, we repacked our bags and prepared for the glacier. Reflecting on the 2008 expedition, I was astounded at how familiar and easy the process now felt after a dozen more expeditions. We packed the tents on the tops of the bags for easy deployment. I did not need to wonder if I had the right equipment; I knew I had exactly what I needed.

It felt like swimming through familiar waters as I checked the forecast and walked over to the taxi service office to finalize our flight. Climbing into Paul Roderick's 1960s supercharged Otter, I sat back and pulled on my headphones. I relaxed as he taxied down the runway and then took off.

I stared out the window at the open bogs and marshes of the Susitna Valley as they passed beneath us. I looked up to the Central Alaska Range. The big three—Denali, Sultana, and Begguya—were there, standing proud as always among the sea of peaks at their base. As we flew, I picked out the Ruth Gorge and the Lacuna, in which Voyager Peak and the Mastodon lurked. The identification of each peak came with a wash of memories.

Then, through the windshield, granite spires dominated the view as Paul pulled the airplane through a small gap between two of the spires. As he circled in on our base camp on the Cul-de-sac Glacier below the northwest face of the shadowed spire, we craned our necks, looking out the windows at the walls as they swept by. He slowly circled down toward the glacier, intentionally providing us magnificent views of the walls around us. The light was flat. Paul gunned the engine in preparation for challenging landing conditions, but instead found hard snow beneath the skis and quickly pulled the craft around 180 degrees before stopping.

We jumped out and stood in the silence of the glacier, looking at the peaks around us. As I scanned the massive proportions of the walls, it was clear that they had not shrunk in the intervening 14 years. In fact, with glacial recession, they were slightly larger than they had been. But instead of looking at them with a sense of wonder and disbelief, my past experience made ascending them now seem possible. Maybe even probable.

"Hell yeah, fellas," I said.

Oliver, having never seen peaks of that proportion, just sat back gaping.

Two days later, Whit and I hung from our third belay on the route and watched as Dave took on the first major blank section of the climb. Closer inspection of the walls had revealed features, but they were incipient and fragile. Dave carefully inspected each flake, moving his body around to get better perspectives on the feature before pulling on it and, if it held, hammering a piton behind it. It was a delicate dance as he moved farther above a ledge.

"Man," I said to Whit, "that looks hard."

Whit nodded. "Yeah, but he's so fast!"

This was modern technical aid climbing, an art mostly learned on the sharp end of El Capitan's hardest routes. I would have been totally out of my depth.

We had truly built a team stronger than any of its parts.

Leaning back, I looked down at our little base camp. Oliver was there, shooting video as the sun arced toward the horizon. We had built out a fortified camp, with tents fully guyed to the glacier and surrounded by walls made from snow blocks. We were ready for a storm, but unlike 14 years before, there was only clear or partly cloudy weather on the horizon.

A major question had been the angle of the wall. Photos made it look either ultrasteep or like a gigantic low-angle slab. Standing at the base, we craned our necks in amazement. The entire wall was slightly overhanging, with the final headwall rearing up behind us, a 2,000-foot wave hanging over our heads.

From the snow at the base, we could see two beautiful and highly visible cracks running straight up, nearly 2,000 feet above us. They taunted us, yet simultaneously begged to be climbed.

At our belay, Whit and I leaned back, looking up.

"If a rock fell off the top, I think it would land well behind us," I predicted.

"Yup," Whit replied, "that's the kind of safety margin I like!" We both chuckled.

Two pitches higher, late in the afternoon, Dave finished his way up an overhanging golden arch that ended with a belay tucked in a corner below a tongue of ice. It was my turn to lead.

As unfamiliar and challenging as the pitch had looked, I felt at home as soon as I swung into the two-inch-thick ice. This was my expertise. It felt wonderful.

I tiptoed up the ice to reach a short snowfield, above which reared a severely overhanging crack that looked like it would take solid gear. Hanging from nylon ladders, I made quick progress as I carefully chose the right piece of protection for each placement. After a few moves, I was able to lean back and look up at the corner above the overhang. It was a winding line of thin ice sprayed into a vertical corner of rock featured with edges and thin cracks.

Hell yeah, this is exactly what I came for.

Eighty feet higher, I was standing on top of a large snow ledge where I built a belay, the upper headwall soaring above me. Up to this point, the wall had been gently overhanging—it was obvious this would continue.

Whit and Dave came up to the belay and we fixed the remainder of our ropes before we rappelled down. This provided us a pathway back to the ground and subsequently back to our high point in the morning. This was part of "Daddy style," our safer and more reasonable method. It gave us the ability to make some progress on the wall while still sleeping in the safety of base camp.

Fixing ropes on the beginning of a route was not a new style—climbers had been doing it for decades. But I had always avoided it in search of a purer style of climbing in which every night of the ascent was spent on the wall. But now, we looked for any opportunity to increase our safety on the route.

Looking up at the wall, Whit said, "We have nothing left to prove other than our continued ability to survive."

Around my neck I wore a medallion depicting Saint Bernard, the patron saint of skiers and alpinists. It was given to me by Julie Kennedy, Hayden's mom, after he passed away. She asked me to wear it while on trips as a token of good luck and a reminder to stay safe. Wearing the necklace from Julie, I intended to keep Hayden and my other lost friends close to my chest as we made decisions. I wanted them there, helping us stay safe in the mountains.

I felt the metal against my chest as we talked about our lost friends as if they were still among us. Kyle and Scott had taken us over the edge in the ethereal realm of the slimmest margins on the hardest walls. Ueli had shown us what it meant to be born to climb. Hayden and Inge had taught us how to love.

We were dedicated to never forgetting the lessons they taught us.

Similarly, those friends who had quit climbing due to the risks or other obligations were afforded the grace of having made good decisions. We discussed their journeys outside of climbing in a celebratory tone.

Our families were equally there with us. We laughed at stories of foibles with our wives, who supported us through our careers both as professionals and as climbers. Unlike generations before, they were not looking after the home front while we, the guys, went to work. Instead, they were driving the charge.

"You know, Shannon's made way more money than me for a long time," I shared. "I think it's great!"

"Better make sure you're doing something to keep her around!" Whit ribbed.

Our fourth day on the glacier, with all our ropes fixed, we rested and prepared to launch. We packed our bags for spending nights on the wall until we reached the summit, while Oliver shot videos and asked questions.

Holding the camera in my face, he asked how I felt.

I stared out at the glacier.

"There's this specific feeling that only comes in this moment, right now, right before a launch. It's this really tight tension between excitement and a little bit of fear and foreboding. It's not a sense of danger, it's a sense of what's to come—the application of power and exertion in this amazing place."

The liminal space before getting into a route used to be uncomfortable. Now it was a good omen.

Early on our fifth day on the glacier, we launched up our fixed lines with alpine climbing and bivouac gear on our backs.

Up to this point, we had been leaving base camp very late. The wall got sun from the early afternoon until nearly midnight, which made for comfortable rock climbing. With nearly 24 hours of light, we didn't need to worry about the typical diurnal cycle of day and night, so we chose when the climbing was best.

Leaving earlier, in hopes of making it to the top of the wall that day, we moved quickly in the cooler air of the morning. We ascended our ropes and pulled them up behind us as we went, committing to the wall.

From the last belay, Whit took the lead and cast off onto the mildly overhanging wall above. Over the course of three hours, he carefully led a sustained 230-foot pitch. Dave then led the two long pitches to the top of the upper headwall.

As he climbed, Whit and I sat back enjoying our location. Dave fought his way up the final few feet of the headwall, well out of sight. We waited patiently.

Suddenly we heard a yell from above and the ropes came tight on the belay, pulling me out of my daze.

"God damn it!" we heard from above. Then, "Are you guys okay?"

Whit and I laughed, looking up at Dave, now hanging on the rope, having taken a 40-foot fall into space.

"Dude! We're supposed to be asking *you* that," Whit yelled.

Dave shook his head as he started to pull back up to his high point. "Good thing this wall is so steep," he yelled back. "Nothing but air on the way down!"

Later, we would find he had made a simple mistake on the final move off the headwall that resulted in a piece of equipment pulling from the wall. "It was dumb, it shouldn't have happened," Dave said, and I knew that he wouldn't let it happen again. All of us had reached this point in our careers not by ignoring our mistakes but by learning from them.

As Dave climbed back up the rope, I thought about how the scenario would have played out if he'd broken an ankle, catching it on a rock flake as he fell, or if he'd broken ribs smashing into a corner. It would have stopped our ascent and it would have been challenging, but we had more than enough equipment and experience to manage an evacuation off the wall.

"This is why we have well-padded safety margins, amigo!" I yelled up the wall. "You're slaying!" Whit and I fist-bumped and smiled. We hadn't missed a beat and we continued upward.

Finally, the terrain leaned back. Whit took the lead and navigated into a short couloir, where he pulled over a chockstone to reach a rib in the snow; from there, we were able to start chopping a ledge into the snow and ice.

We pulled out the tent we had brought, but the ledge was far too small. We laid it out as a ground tarp and slid into our sleeping bags.

"Well, dudes, good thing that the weather's holding," Dave said. "I don't know if I'm going to be able to sleep sitting up in the snow like this."

Ten minutes later, as the sun cast its light from the low point in its arc of the bright Alaskan night, all three of us were sound asleep.

The following morning, I took the lead on the terrain above. Dancing between snow, ice, and rock, I hooked granite edges and swung my tools into ice. I relished in the ability to move quickly on the relatively low-angle terrain. Having left our sleeping kit behind on the ledge below, we were unburdened. I was having fun.

Pulling through a cleft between two ribs of yellow-gold granite, I popped out into the sunshine. Looking up, I could see the ridge above, and after one more pitch, I was on easy ground. Immediately my perspective shifted from the confines of the Cul-de-sac cirque, with base camp situated as a tiny dot, 3,000 feet below. Now my view encompassed the mass of the mountains to the south. I didn't know any of their names, but their steep walls leading to jagged summits represented lifetimes of climbing. Based on our research before the trip, much of it remained unclimbed, ready to offer up adventure.

The guys arrived at the belay in short order. Dave looked out at the ridge of winding, white snow punctuated by gendarmes of granite. "I have always wanted to try climbing this kind of classic alpine terrain," he said before looking at Whit and me. "It's not that hard, right?"

Whit and I both laughed, and I replied, "This *should* be no big deal, but it's most certainly beautiful climbing."

We left behind much of our equipment but kept the rope on as we started climbing. Not wanting to take any chances, we kept pieces of protection between us as we climbed. Whit led the way.

The wind blew over the ridgeline and it felt as if we had launched into outer space. The world was far below. Our umbilical to it was thin, but we were free to move with grace along the ridge. I breathed deeply, embracing that sense of freedom, letting it overwhelm my concerns about the state of humanity and the climate; those were worldly problems, and, for a short moment, I could look down on them from above and not worry.

We were not under any time pressure, but we moved quickly for no reason other than that feeling of freedom. We whooped at each other in the light wind as we sailed over the simple yet extraordinary terrain in a meditative state of flow. Ribs of snow and ledges of ice carried us across the ridgeline as we navigated over and around rock towers. At one point, our way was blocked by a steep downclimb, but Whit spied a tight chimney that we were able to shimmy down to reach a ledge below, from which the path to the summit was clear.

A final arête of firm snow led upward toward the summit block. Whit and Dave, ahead of me, appeared reminiscent of alpinists a generation past, charging up the moderate yet beautiful terrain. And then, in a deft act of route finding, Whit wrapped around the left side of the summit block to a moderate scramble on its far side. He popped out on top, right in front of us, and raised an axe in celebration before quickly bringing in the rope so we could join him.

We all stood on top of Kichatna Spire just after four o'clock in the afternoon.

The top was a patch of snow the size of a large dining room table, and we sat on it, drinking in the views as the sun and wind scraped at our faces. As I looked out at the mountains around us, and thought about how far we had come, a tear came to my eye. I felt the cold medal of Saint Bernard on my chest as a reminder of the friends I would never see again. I took a deep breath, trying not to become too emotional.

I was not alone in my feelings. Next to me, I heard a small sob come from Dave and saw a tear emerge from beneath his sunglasses.

I pulled Dave and Whit together. "Fellas, I love ya."

"Graham, we love you too." Whit embraced me back, with his other arm over Dave's shoulder. "Let's not forget this moment."

Dave leaned into us, taking deep breaths.

"I most certainly will not!" I said. "But hey, we're only halfway done. Let's get the hell out of here safely."

The descent was an exercise in leaning into each other's experience in the mountains. I led us down through the alpine terrain to the top of the wall, where we gathered our equipment from the bivouac. Then we divided responsibilities, with Whit in front, Dave rappelling with the haul bags, and me taking the rear to clean up all our ropes and gear. We were comfortable with our roles and helped each other wherever possible as we tidied up the mountain after our ascent.

By midnight we were back on the ground. We flung our bags from the base of the first pitch to the glacier below. Then we loaded everything onto sleds and sent it sliding back toward base camp, where Oliver awaited our arrival with dinner and cocktails.

Later, Whit looked back up at the route with a celebratory whiskey drink in hand. "That climb was a culmination of over seventy years of experience between the three of us," he said. "That's pretty dang cool."

"It sure is," I replied, clinking his glass.

We were down. We were safe. And after a quick discussion about how the trip should proceed, we called the air taxi and were headed home.

▲

TWENTY-FOUR HOURS LATER, we once again loaded into Paul Roderick's Otter. He had arrived relaxed and enjoying the continued good weather. "In these kinds of conditions," he said, "we get to fly at the pace of comfort."

We all nodded in agreement. Our experience on the wall had felt similar.

The airplane took off and once again Paul circled the spires, clearly enjoying flying in close to these amazing towers of granite rising from the glacier below. Then he pointed the craft down one of the glaciers to the south and followed it out to the open valley.

As we flew, I looked out at the bulk of the Alaska Range as it passed by the oval shape of the airplane window. The familiar mountains moved against each other in a dramatic parallax as we crossed in front of them. The peaks were far away, but the glaciers were just beneath the left side of the airplane as they spilled out onto the valley. I couldn't help but notice their termini, sloped at an angle that demonstrated recession. They were going away. But I tried to look at them with some solace. All is not yet lost, especially if those of us who love these expanses of uplifted rock and ice continue to fight for them.

Watching the terrain pass below us, I realized there would be a last time I would depart from those mountains. A goodbye after which I would never return in person. A point after which I would only visit them in memories.

That range was where my relationship with the world's big mountains had started—it was where I had my first taste of what they had to offer. Those early climbs had cast me on a journey to unbelievable places with incredible people. I had done amazing things in the tens of thousands of hours I had been lucky to spend within their embrace.

Those mountains, cast across the globe, are places I will always love. They will always haunt me. And whether I want to or not, I will always return.

Acknowledgments

I could not have written this memoir without the support and encouragement of many individuals who have played important roles in my life.

Of those whom I need to thank, my wife, Shannon, is first and foremost. She has been my rock throughout my journey as a climber, creative, and advocate. Her patience and understanding have allowed me to pursue this path with a clear mind and a full heart. Shannon, thank you for always believing in me and for being a constant source of inspiration while also being willing to check me when I get out in front of my skis.

I would also like to extend my sincerest gratitude to my parents, Jane and Jeff, and my sister, Greer. While their names don't show up frequently in this book, they have been along for every step of my journey as cheerleaders, confidants, and sounding boards, encouraging me to follow my dreams and pursue my passions, even when I chose to take on the esoteric and dangerous practice of alpinism as my life's work.

To my climbing partners, I owe a debt of gratitude that can never be repaid. They have been my support system and my motivators throughout every climb. Without their expertise and experience, I would not have been able to achieve the things I have in the mountains. Their camaraderie and friendship have made the journey all the more enjoyable, and I am incredibly fortunate to have each of them in my life.

I also feel immense gratitude for Protect Our Winters, the American Alpine Club, and all the other companies and organizations with which I have worked. These groups have enabled me to expand my work beyond what I thought possible.

And thanks to the entire team at the publishing house, particularly the editors with whom I worked on this project; Laura, Tara, Mary, Theresa, Emily, and Kate gave me the tools to develop and polish this manuscript. My thanks also to the designer, Jen, for creating the beautiful cover and design, and to Dede Olson for additional editing assistance. I am grateful for their countless hours of hard work and dedication. Their contributions have been invaluable, and I deeply appreciate the care and attention they gave to this project.

Finally, I would like to express my gratitude to the readers. Your support and interest in my story is humbling and inspiring I hope that my experiences both on and off the mountains encourage you to pursue your own passions. Find out what motivates you and find your own ways to change the world for the better.

About the Author

Professional climber **GRAHAM ZIMMERMAN** is recognized as one of the most acclaimed alpinists of his generation. After graduating in 2007 with a degree in geography, he focused on alpinism, a pursuit that has taken him on more than 40 expeditions and assignments in Alaska, Patagonia, Kyrgyzstan, and Pakistan as well as all over the Lower 48 and Canada. His awards include a 2020 Piolet d'Or, the 2017 Cutting Edge Award for excellence in alpine climbing, and the 2010 New Zealand Alpinist of the Year. Dedicated to using his platform for good, he holds leadership roles in a range of nonprofits and outdoor companies, including the American Alpine Club and Protect Our Winters. He lives in Oregon with his wife, Shannon, and their dog, Pebble.

YOU MAY ALSO LIKE

MY OLD MAN AND THE MOUNTAIN
A Memoir
Leif Whittaker

SIXTY METERS TO ANYWHERE
Brendan Leonard

VALLEY OF GIANTS
Stories from Women at the
Heart of Yosemite Climbing
edited by Lauren DeLaunay Miller

THE ART OF SHRALPINISM
Lessons from the Mountains
Jeremy Jones

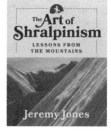

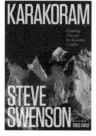

KARAKORAM
Climbing through the Kashmir Conflict
Steve Swenson

THE MOUNTAIN OF MY
FEAR AND DEBORAH: A
WILDERNESS NARRATIVE
Two Mountaineering Classics
David Roberts

www.mountaineersbooks.org

recreation • lifestyle • conservation

MOUNTAINEERS BOOKS, including its two imprints, Skipstone and Braided River, is a leading publisher of quality outdoor recreation, sustainability, and conservation titles. As a 501(c)(3) nonprofit, we are committed to supporting the environmental and educational goals of our organization by providing expert information on human-powered adventure, sustainable practices at home and on the trail, and preservation of wilderness.

Our publications are made possible through the generosity of donors, and through sales of more than 700 titles on outdoor recreation, sustainable lifestyle, and conservation. To donate, purchase books, or learn more, visit us online:

MOUNTAINEERS BOOKS
1001 SW Klickitat Way, Suite 201 • Seattle, WA 98134
800-553-4453 • mbooks@mountaineersbooks.org • www.mountaineersbooks.org

An independent nonprofit publisher since 1960